Baking an Impact

Small Changes For More Sustainable Baking

Baking an Impact

Small Changes For More Sustainable Baking

Genevieve Meli

THE CULINARY INSTITUTE OF AMERICA

Foreward by Eric Ripert

President—Dr. Tim Ryan '77
Provost—Mark Erickson '77
VP of Strategic Initiatives & Branch Campuses—Susan Cussen
Editorial Project Manager—Laura Monroe '12

Interior and cover photography by Phil Mansfield
Book design and illustrations by Scott Citron Design

Published by The Culinary Institute of America Press, Hyde Park, New York

ISBN: 978-1-7320164-1-5

Foreword

THERE IS SOMETHING MAGIC ABOUT the art of pastry. I have never been talented at it, to which, I have been told many times by my family to stick with savory dishes. I have always been fascinated by the immense skill and precision of the craft and have great admiration for pastry chefs.

I had the pleasure of having Chef Genevieve's work in our kitchen at Le Bernardin during the early phases of her career. Since then, she has had many experiences that have led to her success as a pastry chef, now teaching at The Culinary Institute of America.

In this book, she demonstrates her talent while simultaneously focusing on how we can bake smarter to help make an impact. She shows us innovative ways in which we can still create beautiful and delicious sweet and savory pastries, while minimizing waste and creating change. She encourages readers to think outside the box about how small changes to our ingredients, recipes, and techniques can indeed make a positive contribution to our world.

The intention of this book is not to convert you or impose judgement on eating habits, but to inspire bakers of all levels to get creative with their baking, ultimately knowing that adjustments here and there will benefit the well-being of all. With recipes like Wildflower Lollipops and Mirepoix Pot Pie, Chef Genevieve's ideas around baking smarter and more sustainably engage both our palettes and minds for the better.

—CHEF ERIC RIPERT

Contents

Chapter 1: Food Waste

EVERY YEAR, ABOUT 40% OF THE food produced, processed, and transported in the U.S. ends up in the trash. This has dramatic impacts on a large scale, which trickle down to our local communities. Preventing food waste is one of the easiest changes we can make on a daily level.

Imagine the very beginning of the process to grow fresh fruits and vegetables, for instance. Billions of dollars are spent growing and processing the food we buy at the market or grocery store, much of that subsidized by American tax dollars. Add on the monetary cost of disposing of the food that goes unused and imagine what social good that money could do in your community.

According to the National Resource Defense Council, who advocate to defend wildlife, advance climate action, and protect the health of our communities, half of the U.S. land and 80% of the fresh water goes to bringing food to our tables. Wasting our food means wasting these resources, which are already scarce for many people. Every bit of food that we can repurpose means less food in the landfills, but also less money and resources spent replacing it.

Using food waste doesn't mean digging through the garbage to find edible food (though it can and plenty of people do). On a small scale, we can identify the food products that go into our trash cans most often—banana peels, coffee grinds, carrot peels, sour milk—and find a new purpose for what is still edible and full of flavor and nutrients. You'll find some great ideas in this book

One of the culprits to food waste is found in our restaurants, where large portions and garnishes often mean wasted food. Leftovers are great, but not if they don't get eaten, so I encourage professionals and enthusiastic home cooks to scale back just a bit. This isn't about eating less or being on a diet, but more about being realistic about how much food we want and only making enough.

Of course, just because you don't eat something today doesn't mean it has to be discarded right away. I use my freezer for everything, saving little bits and scraps that aren't eaten. Eventually, those items find their way into broths, stews, desserts, breads—anything I can imagine, in they go.

COFFEE COFFEE CAKE

Makes two (8-inch/20-cm) cakes

COFFEE STREUSEL

7.8 oz/220 g all-purpose flour
3.8 oz/109 g brown sugar
Pinch/1 g kosher salt
1.7 oz/50 g coffee grounds
4.6 oz/130 g melted butter

COFFEE CAKE

6 oz/170 g butter
14 oz/400 g sugar
1 tsp/4 g baking powder
¾ tsp/4 g kosher salt
.7 oz/20 g vanilla extract
5.3 oz/150 g eggs
12.3 oz/350 g sour cream
2.1 oz/60 g coffee grinds
9.2 oz/260 g all-purpose flour

If you drink coffee, you have used coffee grounds. There are lots of ways to use them, some you may already know: in your garden or even exfoliating face scrubs. Here, I've used them in a coffee cake that is itself coffee! A little goes a long way, or else the texture can become a bit too grainy. But you can store any leftover used coffee grinds in the freezer for the next time you're craving a cake (or a spa day).

1. For the streusel: in the bowl of a stand mixer fitted with the paddle attachment, combine the flour, sugar, salt, and coffee grounds. Mix to combine.
2. With the mixer on low speed, slowly stream in the butter and mix until just incorporated.
3. Transfer to a sheet pan and refrigerate until firm, at least 30 minutes.
4. For the cake: preheat the oven to 325°F/163°C. Grease two 8-inch/20-cm cake pans.
5. In the bowl of a stand mixer fitted with the paddle attachment, cream the butter and sugar until light and fluffy, scraping the bowl as needed, about 4 minutes.
6. Add the eggs and vanilla in two additions, scraping the bowl down after each. Mix until homogenous.
7. Add the flour, coffee grinds, salt, and baking powder. Mix until the batter is about 75% mixed, then add the sour cream and mix until fully combined.
8. Evenly distribute ¼ of the batter into each prepared cake pan. Evenly distribute the streusel over the cake batter, then top with the remaining batter.
9. Bake until the middle springs back, about 45 minutes.

CHOCOLATE CHIP COOKIE

Makes 15 cookies

Everyone loves a classic chocolate chip cookie, and this one is just a little unique. This recipe calls for Chiffon Flour, which is made from scraps of cake. Depending on the flavors of the cake, it can provide a completely different flavor to the cookies. It may not seem like a huge deal, but using flour from unused ingredients is the kind of small change we can make every day.

1. Preheat the oven to 350°F/175°C.
2. In the bowl of a stand mixer fitted with the paddle attachment, cream the butter and sugars until light and fluffy, about 4 minutes.
3. Add the eggs in four additions, scraping between each. Mix in the vanilla.
4. Sift the flour, baking soda, and salt into the mixing bowl and mix on low speed until almost combined.
5. Add the chocolate chips and mix just to incorporate.
6. Scoop the cookies using a large (3 oz) cookie scoop onto silicone-lined baking sheets.
7. Bake until golden around the edges and the center is just barely soft, about 15 minutes.
8. Transfer to a rack to cool.

7½ oz room temperature unsalted butter
5 oz/213 g granulated sugar
3¼ oz/92 g light brown sugar
3 oz/85 g eggs, room temperature
1 tsp/4 g vanilla extract
10½ oz Chiffon Flour (page 192)
1 tsp/5 g baking soda
1¼ tsp/6 g kosher salt
7 oz/198 g chocolate chips, milk or
  semi-sweet

BISCUIT WITH CORN COB SYRUP

Makes 15 biscuits

9 oz/256 g all-purpose flour
.5 oz/15 g baking powder
1.9 oz/54 g sugar
1 tsp/5 g kosher salt
3.5 oz/100 g lard
9.5 oz/270 g sour heavy cream
Corn kernels, reserved from the syrup
Corn Cob Syrup, for finishing and
  serving (recipe follows)

I really enjoy using soured (not spoiled. Spoiled dairy should be discarded) milk products for a deep, tangy flavor—which is welcome in this scone filled with sweet corn. Rather than finishing with honey, as we so often do with biscuits, I used corn cobs to make a syrup to serve alongside the biscuits. The corn flavor is very powerful and adds a great sweet-and-savory element.

1. Preheat the oven to 350°F/175°C.
2. In a mixer fitted with the paddle attachment, combine the flour, baking powder, sugar, and salt.
3. Add the lard and mix on low speed until walnut-sized pieces form.
4. Add the heavy cream and corn and mix on low speed until just combined.
5. On a floured bench, roll the dough ½" thick.
6. Brush off the excess flour and use a 2½-inch circle cutter to cut the biscuits. Press together any scraps and cut additional biscuits. Transfer the biscuits to a baking sheet and refrigerate for about 20 minutes.
7. Bake until golden brown, about 18 minutes.
8. Remove from the oven and brush with the corn cob syrup while still hot.

CORN ON THE COB SYRUP

Makes about 2 cups/750 g

2 ears of corn, kernels removed and
  reserved for the scones
1 lb 1.5 oz/496 g water
8 oz/227 g sugar
1/2 tsp/2 g kosher salt

1. In a pot, bring the water and corn to a boil. Reduce the heat and simmer for 10 minutes.
2. Remove the corn. Cut the kernels from the cobs and reserve to use in the scones. (The cobs can be dried and used as a firestarter.)
3. To the water, add the sugar and salt, and boil for 10 minutes to reduce slightly.
4. Remove from the heat and set aside to cool to room temperature.

BROCCOLI STEM SCONES

Makes 16 scones

Recipes usually call for broccoli or cauliflower florets, creating lots of leftover trim from the stems of the vegetables. Rather than discard these pieces, which are full of flavor and nutrients, I like to grate them for use in a recipe like these scones. Because they're grated, the tough stems don't have a fibrous mouthfeel, and they'll smell like a delicious quiche. Broccoli and cauliflower are interchangeable here, so use one or both.

1. In the bowl of a stand mixer fitted with the paddle attachment, combine the flour, sugar, baking powder, and salt. Mix on low until just mixed.
2. With the mixer on low speed, add the butter and mix until walnut-sized pieces form. Add the grated broccoli and mix to combine.
3. In a small bowl, combine the eggs, yolks, and cream. Add to the mixer and mix until just combined.
4. Pour the dough out onto a floured surface and roll to 1-inch thick. Brush off any excess flour.
5. Divide the dough in half, and form each half into a circle about 1½-inches thick. Use a chef's knife to cut into eighths.
6. Transfer to a baking sheet and brush with egg wash. Transfer to the refrigerator and chill for at least 20 minutes.
7. Preheat a convection oven to 325°F/160°C. If you do not have a convection oven, preheat to 350°F/175°C.
8. Bake until the edges are browned and the center is soft to the touch, about 12 minutes.
9. Serve warm or at room temperature.

13 oz/368 g pastry flour
1.5 oz/43 g sugar
1 tbsp/14 g baking powder
½ tsp/2 g kosher salt
6 oz/171 g unsalted butter, cubed and chilled
5.1 oz/145 g grated broccoli stem
.9 oz/25 g eggs
.7 oz/20 g egg yolks
7.5 oz/212 g sour heavy cream
Egg Wash (page 196)

AQUAFABA CHIFFON CAKE

Makes three 8-inch cakes

5.6 oz/160 g egg yolks
1 oz/28 g oil
½ tsp/3 g vanilla extract
1 lb 1.6 oz/500 g Chiffon Flour
  (page 192)
9.8 oz/278 g sugar
.7 oz/21 g baking powder
½ tsp/2 g kosher salt
6.8 oz/192 g warm water
8.6 oz/245 g aquafaba
2.8 oz/80 g sugar, plus more as needed
  to prepare the pans
Pinch cream of tartar

Aquafaba is a cornerstone of vegan or plant-forward baking and pastry, made from an ingredient typically washed down the drain. Used most often as a replacement for egg whites, aquafaba is the liquid strained from freshly cooked or canned beans, usually chickpeas. It can be whipped to a foam and even torched like a traditional meringue, without adding any flavor of the bean to the finished item. You'll notice that this cake has blue frosting—for no reason other than a bit of whimsy! I've used blue spirulina, an algae, as a natural food coloring, but you can leave it out if you'd prefer.

1. Preheat a convection oven to 325°F/160°C. If you do not have a convection oven, set the oven to 350°F/175°C.
2. Oil three 8-inch cake pans and dust the pans with sugar; set aside.
3. In the bowl of a stand mixer fitted with the paddle attachment, combine the yolks, oil, and vanilla on medium speed.
4. With the mixer off, sift into the bowl the sugar, baking powder, and salt. Add about half of the water and mix to a paste.
5. Slowly add the remaining water in three stages, scraping the bowl after each addition.
6. Beat on medium speed until well combined and homogenous, about 2 minutes. Transfer to a large bowl.
7. Clean and dry the mixing bowl. Return to the mixer fitted with the whisk attachment. Whip the egg whites with about 1/3 of the sugar and the cream of tartar. Whip until foamy, then sprinkle in the remaining sugar while whipping the meringue to medium peaks.
8. Add the meringue to the egg mixture in 3 stages, folding carefully between each addition.
9. Fill the prepared pans to slightly above halfway.
10. Bake until the cakes are golden brown and spring back when touched, 20 to 30 minutes.
11. Let cool in the pans for a few minutes before turning out onto a cooling rack. Cool completely before filling.
12. To assemble the cake, place one cake layer a cake circle or plate. Pipe the buttercream in a ring on the outside edge of the cake. Fill the circle with about half of the pastry cream.
13. Top the fillings with another layer of cake, and repeat filling with buttercream and pastry cream. Top with the final layer. Use the remaining buttercream to ice the cake all over.

BLUE SPIRULINA SWISS BUTTERCREAM

Makes enough for one 3-layer cake

8 oz/227 g egg whites

1 lb/454 g sugar

1 vanilla bean, scraped

1 lb 8 oz/680 g unsalted butter, room
  temperature, cubed

.5 oz/15 g blue spirulina, or other natural
  food coloring

1. In the bowl of a stand mixer, combine the egg whites and sugar. Place over a pot of simmering water and whisk constantly until the whites reach 140°F/60°C.
2. Place the bowl on the mixer and attach the whisk attachment. Whip on medium-high to form a meringue. Continue mixing until the bowl is only slightly warm to touch, which could take up to 10 minutes or more.
3. Add the butter a few pieces at a time while whipping, incorporating the butter fully after every few additions. Add the vanilla.
4. Turn off the mixer and add the spirulina. Mix very slowly until the powder is incorporated; if you work too quickly, you will make a colorful mess.
5. Transfer to a piping bag fitted with a large round tip.

STONE FRUIT-PIT PASTRY CREAM

Makes enough for one 3-layer cake

1. Combine the eggs, yolks, and cornstarch in a heat-safe bowl. Set aside.
2. In a heavy bottomed pot, bring all the milk and the stone fruit pits to a boil. Remove from the heat, cover, and steep for 40 minutes. Strain and return the milk to the pot.
3. Add the sugar and bring the milk back to a boil. Pour about ½ cup of the hot milk mixture into the bowl with the eggs, whisking constantly to incorporate. Pour this mixture back into the pot, whisking constantly to incorporate.
4. Continue cooking over medium heat, whisking constantly, until the mixture thickens and comes to a boil. Remove from the heat and add the butter. Mix to incorporate.
5. Spread the mixture on a silicone-lined baking sheet or shallow pan to cool. When ready to use, place in a mixing bowl and beat until smooth.

2 whole eggs
4 egg yolks
7.1 oz/200 g stone fruit pits, from peaches, apricots, cherries, etc.
2 lb 1.8 oz/1 L milk
3.5 oz/100 g sugar
1.9 oz/55 g cornstarch
1.8 oz/50 g unsalted butter

BANANA SKIN CREAM TRIFLE

Makes 12 servings

Banana bread is where old bananas go, but what about the skins? Not only are banana skins edible, but they are the perfect consistency for a custard-like cream. The peels on their own can be a little bitter, but we're rounding that out with plenty of sugar and other rich ingredients to balance. Just be sure to scrub the peels before using.

1. Preheat the oven to 325°F/162°C.
2. For the cake: in the bowl of a stand mixer fitted with the paddle attachment, combine the butter and sugar. Cream until homogenous, then add the eggs in three additions.
3. In a small bowl, combine the flour, cocoa powder, salt, and baking soda. Add to the mixing bowl in three additions, alternating with the date pit coffee. Mix until incorporated and homogeous.
4. Divide between two silicone-lined baking sheets. Bake until the cake springs back when lightly pressed, about 20 minutes.
5. Cool fully. Cut into circles, if you like, or into cubes for a more classic presentation. Reserve any cake scraps to make "flour." (see Chiffon Flour, page 192)
6. For the banana cream, bring the banana skins, water, and dates to a boil. Cook until everything is softened, about 15 minutes. Strain, reserving about 1 cup/237 g water.
7. Transfer the banana skins and dates to a blender and purée until smooth, adding water as needed to achieve a custard consistency.
8. To assemble, whip the cream and vanilla sugar to soft peaks.
9. Place a layer of cake at the bottom of a trifle dish, tightly packed. Place additional pieces of cake around the sides of the dish for décor if you like.
10. Place a layer of banana slices over the cake. Add half of the banana cream and spread it over the bananas.
11. Follow with a second layer of cake and bananas. Top with the remaining banana cream, and then spread the whipped cream over top.
12. Top the trifle with another layer of banana slices. Sprinkle with turbinado sugar and use a kitchen torch to brûlée the bananas.
13. If not serving right away, cover tightly and refrigerate for up to 3 days.

DEVIL'S FOOD CAKE

8 oz/227 g unsalted butter
1 lb 9.5 oz/723 g sugar
4 eggs
1 lb 4.5 oz/581 g all-purpose flour
6 oz/170 g cocoa powder
½ tsp/3 g kosher salt
¾ oz/21 g baking soda
24 oz/680 g Date Pit Coffee (page 200)

BANANA SKIN CREAM

8.6 oz/245 g banana skins
5.6 oz/159 g dates, pitted
1 lb 1.6 oz/500 g water
3.5 oz/98 g butter
3.4 oz/96 g banana

ASSEMBLY

10.6 oz/300 g cold heavy cream
1.1 oz/30 g vanilla sugar
6 bananas, sliced into ¼-inch thick coins
Turbinado sugar, as needed for finishing

Instead of discarding used vanilla beans, rinse them, then place them in a low-heat oven to dry. Grind the beans to a smooth powder, and mix with granulated sugar.

SPENT GRAIN CARROT CAKE WITH HONEY ROASTED CARROTS

Makes one 9-in by 13-in cake

CAKE
1 lb 2.3 oz/518 g sugar
11.6 oz/330 g neutral-flavored oil
9 oz/256 g eggs
¾ tsp/4 g kosher salt
12.8 oz/363 g cake flour
.5 oz/14 g baking soda
1½ tsp/4 g ground cinnamon
1½ tsp/4 g ginger powder
17.8 oz/505 g washed and grated carrots
(no need to peel)
7.1 oz/200 g spent grains

CREAM CHEESE FROSTING
11.7 oz/333 g cream cheese
11.7 oz/333 g confectioners' sugar
11.7 oz/333 g unsalted butter, soft

HONEY ROASTED CARROTS
12 mini carrots, tops removed
3.5 oz/100 g honey
1.8 oz/50 g butter, melted

CARROT PURÉE
3.5 oz/100 g carrots, chopped
.4 oz/10 g honey
14.1 oz/400 g water
½ tsp/2 g kosher salt
Honey, as needed for serving

Spent grains are a by-product of alcohol and beer production. They are still full of nutrients with a nutty flavor that is similar, but somehow just a little different than whole grains. I used the spent grains from an IPA brewed at The Culinary Institute of America's on-campus brewery, but you can use whatever is available to you.

1. Preheat the oven to 350°F/175°C. Oil a 9 – by 13-inch baking pan and set aside.
2. In the bowl of a stand mixer fitted with the whisk attachment, combine the sugar, oil, eggs, and salt. Combine on medium speed.
3. In a separate, sift together the flour, baking soda, cinnamon, and ginger. Add to the wet ingredients and mix to combine.
4. Add the carrot and spent grains and mix until incorporated and homogenous.
5. Spread the batter into the prepared pan. Bake until the cake is golden brown and springs back when pressed lightly, about 45 minutes.
6. Meanwhile, for the cream cheese frosting, combine the cream cheese and confectioners' sugar in the bowl of a stand mixer fitted with the paddle attachment. Mix until smooth, scraping the bowl as needed. Add the butter and mix until the frosting is very smooth. Set aside until needed.
7. Preheat the oven to 400°F/200°C.
8. For the honey roasted carrots, use a knife to score the carrots to about halfway through. Transfer to a roasting pan. Add the honey and butter, and roll the carrots to coat.
9. Cover the pan with foil and transfer to the oven. Bake until tender, about 15 minutes. Set aside to cool.
10. For the carrot purée, combine the carrots, honey, water, and salt in a saucepan. Cook over medium-high heat until tender, about 10 minutes. Use a slotted spoon to transfer the carrots to a blender and purée, using some of the cooking liquid as needed to facilitate blending while keeping a scoopable consistency. (The remaining cooking liquid can be used to water plants.)
11. Turn the cake out onto a clean surface and cut into 5-inch wide strips. Top each strip with 3.5 oz/100 g of the frosting and spread until it is smooth. Stack the layers one on top of another to form a layer cake. Refrigerate for at least two hours or overnight.
12. When you're ready to serve, cut the cake into ½-inch slices. Turn the slices on their side and cut with a round cutter (choose the size that best utilizes the majority of the cake).
13. To assemble, spoon a dollop of carrot purée on the bottom of a serving plate and spread organically. Place the cake round over the purée, and top with the roasted carrots. Drizzle with honey before serving.

MIREPOIX POT PIE

Makes one 10-inch pie

In preparing stocks, broths, and some other dishes like roasts and braises, there is often discarded aromatic vegetables that were used to flavor the base of the dish that are not served along with it. Called mirepoix, this mix of onion, carrot, celery, and garlic is still full of life, even after cooking. Here, I've blended the vegetables from a vegetable stock to create a savory filling for a pot pie, but you can use this same principle with any mix of cooked vegetables. If they come from a roast or other "dry-heat" cooking method, you may need to add some stock or water to blend.

1. On a floured surface, roll the 11 oz/312 g puff pastry to fit a 10-inch-deep dish pie plate. Transfer to the pie plate and refrigerate until needed.
2. With the 24 oz/680 g puff pastry, roll to a rectangle that is approximately 5 – by 24-inches/13 – by 61-cm. Spread the tomato jam across the top of the pastry.
3. With the long side facing your body, roll the dough like a jellyroll from the bottom to the top. Cut in half, transfer to a baking sheet, and freeze until firm enough to slice, at least 10 minutes.
4. Slice the roll ¼-inch/6 mm thick to make spiral disks. Return to the baking sheet and freeze until needed.
5. Preheat the oven to 425°F/218°C.
6. Blend the cooked mirepoix and add to a blender with salt and onion powder. Add a splash of water or stock to facilitate blending, if needed. Pour into the chilled pastry-lined pie plate and spread evenly.
7. In a skillet over medium-high heat, melt the tallow. Add the onion and celery, and sauté until the onions are translucent, 3 to 5 minutes. Add the carrots and garlic, and sauté until aromatic, another 1 to 2 minutes.
8. Sprinkle the vegetables with the flour and stir to coat. Cook for 1 to 2 minutes, stirring constantly. We simply want to cook out the raw flavor of the flour, but we don't want to develop any color.
9. Add the stock and stir to dissolve the flour, scraping any bits on the bottom of the pan.
10. Season with salt and pepper, to taste. Add the peas and herbs and remove from the heat.
11. Transfer to the pie plate, covering the vegetable purée. Arrange the chilled pastry spirals over the top of the filling, shingling as needed to cover. Brush with egg wash.

1. In a saucepan over medium heat, combine the tomatoes and 3.5 oz/100 g of the sugar. Bring to a boil.
2. In a small bowl, stir together the pectin powder and remaining 25 g/.9 oz sugar. Stir the pectin mixture into the tomatoes.
3. Add the lemon juice and remove from the heat. Set aside to cool fully before using.

2 lb 3 oz/992 g Tallow Puff Pastry ("Tallow Puff Pastry" on page 199), divided into 2 pieces: 11 oz/312 g for the bottom layer and 1 lb 8 oz/680 g for the top layer
Tomato Jam (recipe below)
Egg Wash (page 196), as needed

14 oz/400 g reserved mirepoix
Kosher salt, to taste
1 tsp/4 g Onion Powder (page 202)

1 oz/28 g beef tallow or other cooking fat as preferred
1 medium onion, chopped
2 stalks celery, chopped
2 medium carrots, chopped
5 large cloves garlic, chopped
5.3 oz/150 g all-purpose flour
2 cups/470 mL stock
3.5 oz/100 g peas
.3 oz/9 g chopped thyme leaves
.4 oz/10 g chopped rosemary leaves
.3 oz/8 g chopped sage leaves
Kosher salt, to taste
Freshly ground black pepper, to taste

TOMATO JAM
10.6 oz/300 g tomatoes, chopped
4.4 oz/125 g sugar, divided use
1.8 oz/50 g lemon juice
1/2 oz/15 g apple pectin powder

DANISH PIE

Makes one 10-inch pie

2 Spelt Pie Crusts (page 180), divided
    in two pieces
4.2 oz/120 g brown sugar
14 oz/397 g Date Pit Coffee (page 200)
Zest from 5 lemons
Juice from 5 lemons
11.3 oz/320 g prepared Danish, roughly
    chopped
.4 oz/10 g kosher salt
2.8 oz/80 g unsalted butter, cut into small
    cubes
Egg Wash (page 196)

I made the Depression-era cracker pie, where crackers are used in place of apples for a surprisingly similar flavor. I was inspired. So, when I spotted uneaten Danish going to waste at work (everyone was tired of the bread pudding we usually made), my first thought was "Put it in a pie!" Because Danish are typically filled with ingredients like fruits, nuts, or cheese, they added a lot of flavor to the pie, which was very moist and really delicious. In my experiments, I found that very stale Danish worked just as well as day-old.

1. Roll out one pie dough to fit a 10-inch pie plate, and reserve in the refrigerator. Roll the second pie dough to 11-inches. Cut a hole in the center and 6 vents to release steam during baking. Transfer to the refrigerator to chill.
2. Preheat the oven to 400°F/204°C.
3. In a saucepan, bring the brown sugar and date pit coffee to a boil over moderate heat. Boil until the liquid is reduced by about half, about 5 minutes. Remove from the heat.
4. In a heat-safe bowl, combine the lemon zest, juice, Danish, and salt. Pour the reduced coffee over the ingredients in the bowl and mix to combine.
5. Pour into the prepared pie crust. Dot the filling with the cubed butter.
6. Brush the edges of the shell with egg wash and place the top pie crust over the filling. Press the sides of the crust so they adhere together. Trim the edges and crimp or press with a fork to seal. Egg wash the top of the pie.
7. Transfer to the oven and bake until the crust is golden brown and fully baked, about 30 minutes.
8. Place on a rack to cool completely before slicing and serving.

VINEGAR CUSTARD

Makes 8 to 10 servings

Vinegar pie was a popular recipe during the Great Depression, when people had little to use and made what they could. Made with just a few ingredients, this pie was smooth and silky, with the unmistakable tang of vinegar. This custard is inspired by vinegar pie, using homemade Apple Cider Vinegar (page 192). There's still a subtle bite from the vinegar, but there's still space for the floral notes of the apples in the vinegar.

7.1 oz/200 g eggs
7.4 oz/213 g brown sugar
.6 oz/17 g Apple Cider Vinegar (page 192)
1 tsp/5 g kosher salt
2.8 oz/80 g unsalted butter

1. Preheat the oven to 350°F/175°C.
2. In a large bowl, combine the eggs, brown sugar, vinegar, and salt. Whisk to combine. Stream in the melted butter and whisk until incorporated.
3. Pour into a greased 8-inch cast iron skillet or other heavy baking pan.
4. Bake until the custard is set around the edges and jiggles in the center, about 20 minutes.
5. Cool before serving.

WHEY CRULLER

Makes 13 crullers

8 oz/227 g whey
3 oz/85 g butter
1 tsp/3 g kosher salt
5 oz/145 g all-purpose flour
2½ tsp/10 g sugar
2 oz/60 g whole eggs
2 oz/60 g egg whites

Whey is a by-product of the cheese making process, typically discarded. In addition to being a flavorful liquid with many sweet or savory uses, whey contains proteins, amino acids, and other nutrients. I've used it in these crullers like you might use buttermilk in another batter, for a little tang and a tender dough.

1. Combine the whey, butter, and salt into a medium saucepan. Bring to a full boil, then remove from the heat and add all the flour at once. Stir with a wooden spoon until homogenous.
2. Return to medium-low heat. Stir constantly until a film forms at the bottom of the pot.
3. Transfer the hot mixture to a 5-quart mixer fitted with the paddle attachment. Mix on low speed for about 30 seconds until slightly cooled.
4. Add the eggs and whites in four additions, beating just until incorporated between each addition.
5. Transfer the batter to a pastry bag fitted with an 806 tip.
6. Pipe in 3-inch circles, about 45 grams each, on parchment paper squares.
7. Preheat frying oil to 375°F/190°C. Carefully place the crullers, dough-side down, into the hot oil. The parchment paper will release from the cruller and can be removed with a spoon.
8. Fry the crullers, flipping as needed, until golden brown on both sides, 1½ to 2 minutes.
9. Remove from the oil and transfer to a cooling rack. Once cooled, dunk in the glaze and set on a wire rack to set.

4.3 oz/122 g whey
7 oz/200 g confectioners' sugar
½ oz/15 g lemon zest

WHEY GLAZE

Makes enough for 13 crullers

1. Combine the whey, sugar, and zest. Mix until smooth. Store covered in the refrigerator until needed.

PINEAPPLE TEA JELLO

Makes 8 servings

Spiky and tough, pineapple skins are almost always relegated to the trash or compost. If you have ever nibbled one on, you know that they have an incredible pineapple flavor, so naturally, I made a tea. You can use the tea on its own, but I really enjoy this jello to eat as is or as part of a dessert.

3 lb .7 oz/1382 g water

2 lb 5.9 oz/1074 g pineapple skin

4.6 oz/130 g sugar

1.1 oz/30 g gelatin sheets, soaked in ice water and strained

1. Bring the water to a boil in a medium saucepan. Add the pineapple skin and remove from the heat. Cool, then cover and refrigerate overnight.
2. Strain and discard the peels. Return the pineapple tea to a boil and add the sugar. Stir to dissolve.
3. Remove from the heat and add the hydrated gelatin. Stir until melted.
4. Pour into heat-safe glasses, jars, or another container. Refrigerate overnight to set.
5. Serve in the vessel or run under warm water to unmold.

SQUID INK BRIOCHE

Makes four 9 – by 5-inch loaves

6.3 oz/180 g whole milk
6.6 oz/187 g eggs
1 lb 1.7 oz/500 g bread flour
1.5 oz/43 g sugar
.4 oz/11 g instant yeast
.4 oz/10 g milk powder
.5 oz/14 g kosher salt
5.5 oz/157 g unsalted butter, cold
1 oz/25 g squid ink

I am a believer that if you're going to go through the effort to make brioche, it's worth making extra to freeze for a rainy day. If you don't have four loaf pans, you can bake it in batches. Divide the dough into four pieces and leave the dough yet-to-be-baked in the refrigerator until it's time. You can also bake the bread in other similar-sized pans. This recipe uses squid ink for a dramatic result. Used sparingly, it gives the bread a beautiful, mild flavor—but a little goes a long way, so resist the urge to add more.

1. In the bowl of a stand mixer fitted with a dough hook, combine the milk and eggs. Add the bread flour, sugar, yeast, milk powder, and salt, and mix on low speed to incorporate, for about 4 minutes.
2. Increase the speed to medium and mix until the dough reaches the right stage of gluten development, about 8 minutes. To check for gluten development, take a piece of dough and stretch it very gently. If you can see light through the window that forms, you are ready to move on to the next step. If it breaks easily, let it mix a little longer. This depends on the strength of your mixer, so it may take longer.
3. With the mixer on medium speed, add the butter a little at a time. Continue mixing until the butter is all incorporated and the dough is homogenous. Add the squid ink and mix just until fully combined.
4. Transfer the dough to an oiled bowl and set aside to ferment until the dough has doubled in size. This is very dependent on the temperature of your dough and the environment, and could take an hour or more.
5. Punch the dough down in the bowl, then cover and refrigerate overnight.
6. On a floured work surface, divide the dough into 10.5 oz/300 g pieces and shape into oblongs about the same length as your loaf pans.
7. Grease the loaf pans, then transfer the dough to the pans.
8. Set in a warm, humid place until doubled in size, anywhere from 1 to several hours, depending on the environment.
9. Preheat the oven to 350°F/175°C.
10. Bake until the loafs feel set and the internal temperature reaches 200°F/93°C, about 40 minutes.
11. Turn the bread out onto a cooling rack. Cool completely before slicing.

SOUR MILK PANCAKES WITH CANDIED PINECONES

Makes 6 servings

Soured milk is an ingredient most of us have at some point, probably more frequently than we care to admit. Different than spoiled (which would smell like blue cheese, versus just a little tangy), soured milk is a safe ingredient to add the sour flavor we're used to from buttermilk or sour cream. I've paired these pancakes with pinecone syrup (and tasty little pinecones), for a flavor that is a little nutty, but also tastes a bit like a pine tree smells. I love it, and it uses an abundant natural resource. Pick the pinecones early in the season (March, in the northeast United States), when they are very small and still green.

7.1 oz/200 g all-purpose flour
1 tsp/5 g kosher salt
.5 oz/15 g baking powder
1.8 oz/50 g maple sugar
1.9 oz/55 g unsalted butter, melted, plus more as needed for cooking
.7 oz/20 g vanilla paste or extract
3.5 oz/100 g eggs
8.8 oz/250 g sour milk
Candied Pinecones (*recipe follows*)

1. In a mixing bowl, whisk together the flour, salt, and baking powder. Add the sugar, butter, vanilla, eggs, and sour milk, and whisk until smooth.
2. Butter a pan over medium heat. Once hot, ladle the pancake batter into the pan. Flip once small bubbles form on the surface of the pancake, about 1 minute.
3. Flip the pancake and cook until golden brown on the second side, about 1 minute more.
4. Remove to a plate and continue cooking until you've used all the batter.
5. Serve with candied pinecones in their syrup.

CANDIED PINECONES

Makes about 1 quart

2.6 oz/73 g pinecones
2 lb 3.2 oz/1 kg water
10.6 oz/300 g sugar

1. Combine the pinecones, water, and sugar in a pot and bring to a boil over moderate heat.
2. Reduce to a simmer. Cook until the pinecones are tender and brown, about 1 hour.
3. Set aside to cool slightly, and store in the syrup.

SOUR CRUMBLE CHOCOLATE MARBLE BARS

Makes about 12 chocolate bars, depending on size

SOUR POWDER

3.5 oz/100 g whole wheat sour

½ tsp/5 g kosher salt

4.4 oz/125 g sugar

4.4 oz/125 g all-purpose flour

3.5 oz/100 g melted butter

8.8 oz/250 g dark chocolate, tempered, or as needed

8.8 oz/250 g white chocolate, tempered, or as needed

A well-maintained sourdough starter can be a baker's most prized possession—sometimes more like a member of the family! Part of that process often means discarding some of your starter and then feeding it with fresh flour and water, which is a little heartbreak every time. Luckily, your discarded sourdough starter can be used in any number of items, like flatbreads, pancakes, and yes, even chocolate bars! I've dehydrated here to concentrate the flavor, and I've paired it with dark and milk chocolate for a textured, marbled candy bar.

1. To prepare the sour powder, spread the sour on a silicone-lined baking sheet. Set your oven to its lowest heat setting. Leave the sour to dry out in the low oven, with the door ajar, if possible, until completely dry, ideally overnight. Alternately, use a dehydrator.

2. Transfer the sour to a food processor and grind until somewhat smooth, but not a fine powder. Set aside.

3. Preheat the oven to 350°F/177°C.

4. To the food processor with the sour powder, add the sugar and flour and blend to incorporate. Add the butter in a steam stream and pulse until the mixture forms crumbs.

5. Transfer the crumbs to a baking sheet. Bake until crispy and golden brown, about 12 minutes. Set aside to cool completely.

6. Place the dark chocolate in a bowl. To the same bowl, gently pour in the white chocolate. Agitate gently to lightly swirl the chocolate together, but do not mix.

7. Gently pour the chocolate into your preferred chocolate molds. Placed the cooled crumble throughout the chocolate, and cover with another layer of marbled chocolate. Tap the molds against a hard surface to release any air bubbles.

8. Allow to set fully before unmolding. Use stencils to add decorative tempered chocolate to the surface, if you would like.

SOUR BROWN BUTTER CANDLES

Makes 2 to 4 candles, depending on size and shape

By now you have seen plenty of ways to use spoiled milk, but this one is just a little different. These butter candles (yes, real candles!) are made using sour dairy products for a great flavor. As they melt, so does the butter, which you can scoop up with bread, crackers, radishes, and anything that tastes better with butter—so, everything. These are a lot of fun for a party or shared plate. I used an 8 oz candle mold, but you can make yours in whatever shape and size you like.

1. Place two 9-in by 13-in pans and a bowl of ice water in the freezer. Prepare a strainer set over a bowl and set aside.
2. Combine the crème fraîche and cream in the bowl of a stand mixer fitted with the paddle attachment. Mix on high speed until the mixture separates, with a milky liquid surrounding a yellow mass.
3. Remove from the mixer and knead in the bowl to form a ball. Strain out any liquid.
4. Add the ice-cold water to the bowl and knead again to "wash" the solids.
5. Remove from the bowl and transfer to the baking pans, dividing among the two. Press the butter with your hands or another flat tool to remove as much water as possible. Discard any liquid and continue to press one more time to remove any excess water.
6. Allow the butter to warm up and soften. Add the brown butter solids and mix until smooth. It should be soft. Transfer to a piping bag.
7. At the bottom of your candle mold, place a round wick holder and attack the corn wick. Pipe the butter into the molds. Refrigerate until firm.
8. Unmold the candles. They are now ready to use.

1 lb/454 g soured crème fraîche
2 lb 1.7 oz/954 g soured heavy cream
4 oz/113 g brown butter solids

Wick holders, as needed
Corn Wicks (recipe below), as needed

When browning butter, a white foam will form at the top of the butter. I take this foam and place it in a pot. Cook on medium heat, stirring constantly, until the solids brown. Strain and cool, then use in this recipe and others.

CORN HUSK WICKS

Makes enough for at least 4 candles

1. Tear the husks into strips that are roughly the same size. They should be about 2-inches longer than your candle mold. Take two of the strips and knot them together at the top, then twist each strip away from you, and then twist together.
2. Set the wicks aside to dry for a day or two. If they are still green, let them dry longer.
3. Melt the wax and dip each husk into the wax. Dip the husk in the wax and set aside to set until ready for use.

1 corn husk
Bees wax, as needed

DUCK FAT POPCORN

Makes 4 to 6 portions

2.1 oz/60 g duck fat

14.1 oz/400 g popcorn kernels

.9 oz/25 g Onion Powder (page 202), plus as needed

2.6 oz/75 g clarified butter milk solids, plus more as needed

.5 oz/15 g kosher salt, plus more as needed

In the food world, adding duck fat to a simple ingredient is an instant upgrade. I've combined the duck fat with clarified milk solids for a savory and rich popcorn.

1. Melt the duck fat in a large pot over high heat. Add the kernels and cover tightly with a lid.
2. Gently shake the pot to distribute the kernels. The kernels will begin to pop. Continue cooking until the popping has slowed. Remove from the heat.
3. Add the butter solids, onion powder, and salt. Mix to combine and adjust with additional seasonings to taste.

CHOCOLATE-COATED CHEESE RINDS

Makes about 20 pieces

I love cheese. I just do, and I am happy to enjoy it in any number of ways. Since cheese-making is a very expensive and time-consuming process, I hate to let anything go to waste. Once you've finished a block of hard cheese, you're left with the rind, which we often use to flavor broths or soup—but how much broth can you have in your freezer for a rainy day? These cheese rinds are crispy with a beautiful, concentrated flavor, which is incredible alongside the chocolate and sea salt.

2 lb 3.3 oz/1 kg rinds from Parmesan or any other hard cheese

7.1 oz/200 g tempered milk chocolate, or milk chocolate coating chocolate, melted

Maldon salt, as needed for finishing

1. Preheat the oven to 425°F/220°C.
2. Cut the cheese rinds into strips. Place on a rack set over a baking sheet, and bake until the rinds are puffed and bubbly, about 15 minutes. Remove from the oven and set aside to cool fully.
3. Place the chocolate in a bowl. Dip the rinds, leaving some exposed rind to hold, and sprinkle with salt. Set aside until the chocolate sets.
4. Store at room temperature in a covered container.

CANDIED WATERMELON RIND

Makes about 3 quarts

2 lb 3.3 oz/1 kg water

3 lb 4.9 oz/1500 g granulated sugar

1 used vanilla bean, or about 1 tsp/5 mL
vanilla extract

5 strips of lemon peel, peeled with a
vegetable peeler or knife

3 oz/85 g lemon juice

Rind from 1 large watermelon, cut into
1-inch pieces

Watermelon rinds are usually a picnic casualty, occasionally finding their way to some brine to become pickles. Instead of pickling, I like to candy the rinds for a sweet little bite that you can enjoy out of hands or served alongside other desserts. They are a refreshing treat on a hot day. When cutting the watermelon, I like to keep a small strip the flesh on to make it look even prettier.

1. In a large saucepot, bring the water, sugar, vanilla, lemon peel, and lemon juice to a boil.
2. Add the watermelon rind and bring to a simmer. Cook until tender, and translucent, about 30 minutes.
3. Cool fully before transferring the rinds and liquid to covered containers. Store in the refrigerator for up to 6 months.

APPLE CIDER VINEGAR POSSET WITH SPECULOOS CRUMBS AND APPLE BUTTER

Makes 4 servings

When apples skins are abundant, I always use them to make Apple Cider Vinegar (page 192), which is the perfect acidic element to a simple posset. Possets are made from milk and sometimes sugar "curdled" with an acidic ingredient, like lemon juice or vinegar, to create a silky-smooth custard. In the theme of waste-not-want-not, I baked some crispy cookies using fresh breadcrumbs in place of flour to crush as a crumbly garnish.

1. For the posset, place sugar, heavy cream, and salt in a pot on high heat. Bring to boil for 2 minutes
2. Add cider vinegar and stir to combine. Remove from the stove.
3. Pour into 4 heat-safe bowls, ramekins, or other individual serving vessels. Cover and refrigerate overnight.
4. For the breadcrumbs, in the bowl of a stand mixer fitted with the paddle attachment, cream the butter and brown sugar, scraping as needed, until light and fluffy, about 4 minutes.
5. With the mixer on low speed, stream in the milk and vanilla. Scrape the bowl as needed.
6. Add the breadcrumbs, baking soda, and baking powder, and mix until combined.
7. Transfer to a silicone mat on a clean work surface, and roll to about 1/8-inch. Refrigerate for at least 1 hour.
8. Preheat the oven to 325°F/160°C.
9. Cut the chilled dough into rough squares on the baking sheet. Transfer to the oven and bake until browned and crisp, about 10 minutes. Remove from the oven and set aside to cool fully.
10. Transfer the cookies to a food processor and grind to a powder.
11. Meanwhile, roll the puff pastry to ¼-inch thick and freeze to semi-frozen. Cut into ⅓-inch/1 cm strips.
12. Cook the pastry in a hot sandwich press or griddle set at about 400°F/200°C until golden brown and crisp, about 1 minute. Alternately, you can bake the strips in a 350°F/175°C oven for a few minutes. Set aside to cool.
13. To assemble, place the apple butter in a piping bag and pipe it over half of the posset. Cover the apple butter with apple ribbons. Sprinkle the breadcrumbs into the folds of the apple ribbons and top the dessert with two strips of puff pastry.

POSSET
3 oz/84 g sugar
9.7 oz/276 g heavy cream
Pinch of kosher salt
2 oz/57 g lightly aged (2 to 4 weeks) cider vinegar

SPECULOOS BREADCRUMBS
5.9 oz/166 g unsalted butter, room temperature
10 oz/283 g light brown sugar
3.4 oz/96 g milk
1 tsp/5 g vanilla
12.2 oz/346 g fresh breadcrumbs
3.5 oz/99 g almond powder
.5 oz/13 g baking soda
2 apples, peeled and cut into thin ribbons with a vegetable peeler
1 cup/300 g apple butter
4 oz/113 g Beef Tallow Puff Pastry (page 199)

PAVLOVA WITH PICKLED STRAWBERRIES, OLIVE-PIT CHANTILLY, AND FRIED STRAWBERRY TOPS

Makes two 8-inch cakes

.9 oz/26 g corn starch
½ tsp/2 g kosher salt
11.5 oz/327 g sugar
6.2 oz/175 g egg whites
1½ tsp/5 g cream of tartar
.6 oz/16 g vanilla paste
1.8 oz/52 g almond flour

Olive-Pit Cream (recipe below)
Pickled Strawberries (recipe below)
Snap dragons, for garnish (optional)

Though store-bought almond flour works great here, I like making my own from the byproduct of making almond milk.

After making the milk, you'll have lots of pulp. Spread that on a baking sheet and toast it until it is dry and fragrant.

Olives are a staple in my house, and I have always felt terrible throwing away the pits. Infused in the cream, they bring a mild savory quality that I really enjoy with bright fresh fruits like strawberries. Of course, we use the tops of the strawberries for a crisp garnish, and I used my own almond flour, made from the pulp leftover from making almond milk, to give structure to the pavlova.

1. Preheat the oven to 285°F/140°C.
2. Lightly oil two 8-inch cake pans. Line with parchment paper circles. Set aside.
3. In a small bowl, mix the corn starch, salt, and sugar. Set aside.
4. In the bowl of a stand mixer fitted with the whisk attachment, combine the egg whites, cream of tartar, and vanilla. Whip on high speed until the egg whites have tripled in volume. Lower to medium speed and slowly stream in the corn starch mixture.
5. Continue whipping until the mixture is about 8 times its original volume and stiff peaks form, about 8 minutes.
6. Remove from the mixer and fold in the almond flour. Spread in the prepared pans.
7. Bake until dry and crisp, about 50 minutes.
8. Cool fully in the pans, then run a knife around the sides of the pan and turn out onto a plate. Flip again so the top is facing up.
9. Spoon a dollop of olive chantilly on a serving plate. Place the pavlova on the chantilly to secure to the plate.
10. Spoon more of the chantilly over the pavlova and top with pickled strawberries, fried strawberry tops, and snap dragons, if you like.

OLIVE-PIT CHANTILLY

Makes enough for two 8-in cakes

1 lb 1.6 oz /500 g heavy cream
16 Castelvetrano olive pits
.5 oz/10 g sugar

1. In a covered container, combine the cream and olive pits. Refrigerate to infuse for 48 hours.
2. Strain the cream into a bowl and add the sugar. Whip until soft peaks form. Refrigerate until ready to use.

PICKLED STRAWBERRIES

Makes enough for two 8-inch cakes

1.8 oz/50 g honey
5.3 oz/150 g Apple Cider Vinegar
 (page 192)
5.3 oz/150 g water
10.6 oz/300 g strawberries, hulled, sliced,
 tops reserved for garnish

Vegetable oil, as needed for frying
Sugar, as needed

1. In a covered container, combine the honey, vinegar, and water. Add the strawberries and refrigerate for 24 hours.
2. Strain the strawberries for the liquid when ready to use. Reserve the liquid to use for a vinaigrette.
3. In a medium pot, heat the oil to 275°F/135°C. Add the strawberry tops and fry for about 5 seconds. Use a slotted spoon to remove to a towel-lined pan and immediately sprinkle with sugar.

Chapter 2: Alternative Ingredients

WHILE I LOVE EXPERIMENTING with new ingredients, one of the primary reasons for using alternative ingredients is to accommodate special diets. This can include vegan, dairy-free, gluten-free, allergen-free, kosher, and heart-healthy, to name only a few. Knowing what is in our ingredients, what their purpose is in a recipe, and how to manipulate those ingredients is a key skill when baking for special diets.

Since grains are used in so many baking products, understanding the difference between flours can help you make the right choices in choosing ingredients. Standard all-purpose flour, along with the other major commercial flours including whole wheat, is made with a variety of wheat called common wheat or bread wheat. This wheat contains gluten proteins that give breads, cookies, and other baked goods structure. Gluten-free grains, like rice, corn, millet, and buckwheat, can be milled into flours to provide nutritious alternatives for those with intolerance or sensitivity.

Vegan baking, where no animal products or byproducts are used, can act as a greater umbrella for other special diets, like dairy-free and egg-free. Replacing dairy products like milk, butter, and cheese is becoming increasingly easy, with a wide availability of prepared non-dairy ingredients. Though some are less processed than others, it is important to read the ingredients on these products, since vegan does not equal healthy. Look first to whole ingredients to replace ingredients. Instead of commercial non-dairy ice cream, look to nuts, oats, and plant-based thickeners like tapioca starch to create creamy vegan ice cream. Instead of a commercial egg substitute, make your own Flax Paste (page 195) to use in place of whole eggs.

When it comes to baking, sugar is a hot topic: should we consume any sugar at all? What sugars are better than others? This is certainly not a health book, as you can see from recipes like Chocolate-Covered Cheese Rinds (page 39) and Whey Crullers (page 24), but in the spirit of making small changes, I like introducing some "better" sugars to balance the less nutrient-dense ingredients in our desserts. Natural sweeteners like honey, real maple syrup, and agave nectar are still sugar, but they are less processed—good for us and the environment—and many have lower glycemic loads and more nutrients. I still use sugar in plenty of recipes because it has properties that are ideal for baking. But, when I can use something different to make small changes, I do.

LEMON BALM OLIVE OIL CAKE

Makes two 8-inch cakes

1.8 oz/50 g eggs
2.6 oz/73 g egg yolks
10.6 oz/300 g sugar
Zest of 1 lemon
10.8 oz/307 g extra-virgin olive oil
13.2 oz/375 g cake flour
¾ tsp/5 g baking soda
½ tsp/2 g baking powder
¾ tsp/3 g kosher salt
2 tsp/8 g dried lemon balm, plus more
  for garnish
7.8 oz/220 g buttermilk
4.1 oz/115 g milk
Honey, as needed for finishing

Olive oil is delicious in its own right, but it also happens to be a more heart-healthy and earth-friendly alternative to butter. Olive trees trap more carbon than they release, which is not true for the dairy cows we rely on for butter. The olive oil flavor in this cake is not overwhelming or savory, but it adds a different and unique richness over sweet butter. This recipe makes two cakes, so freeze one for later, if you like.

1. Preheat the oven to 325°F/160°C. Oil two 8-inch cake pans.
2. In a large bowl, combine the eggs, yolks, sugar, and lemon zest. Whisk until the mixture has thickened slightly and is pale yellow in color, about 4 minutes.
3. Stream in the olive oil while whisking constantly. Whisk until homogenous.
4. Add half the dry ingredients and stir to combine. Add the buttermilk, and mixto combine.
5. Add the remaining dry ingredients and mix until incorporated, then add the milk and mix to combine.
6. Divide the batter between the prepared cake pans.
7. Bake until the center of the cake springs back when pressed, about 20 minutes.
8. Transfer to a rack to cool. Drizzle with honey and fresh lemon balm before serving.

ZUCCHINI BLACKBERRY BREAD

Makes 1 bundt cake

This bread (which is honestly a cake) is so full of zucchini that you can maybe call it a salad! To me, though, the star of this zucchini bread is the flax seed paste that takes the place of eggs. Egg processing is a huge contributor to carbon emissions, as opposed to flax—which has the added benefit of being nutritious.

1. Preheat the oven to 350°F/175°C. Oil a bundt or ring pan; set aside (you can also use individual sized bundt pans, but baking time will vary).
2. In a large mixing bowl, combine the flax seed paste, sugar, brown sugar, oil, water, and vanilla. Add the flours, salt, baking soda, baking powder, and nutmeg. Stir to combine.
3. Fold in the zucchini and blackberries.
4. Pour the batter into the prepared pan.
5. Bake until the cake is golden brown and the center bounces back when touched, about 35 minutes.
6. Cool in the pan for about 15 minutes before turning out onto a cooling rack.
7. Cool completely before garnishing with blackberries and flowers, if using.

4.7 oz/133 g Flax Seed Paste (page 195)
4.6 oz/130 g granulated sugar
4.1 oz/115 g brown sugar
5.2 oz/147 g vegetable oil
2.8 oz/80 g water
.5 oz/15 g vanilla
5.5 oz/155 all-purpose flour
2.5 oz/70 g hazelnut flour
¾ tsp/4 g kosher salt
½ tsp/3 g baking soda
½ tsp/2 g baking powder
½ tsp/1 g grated nutmeg
10 oz/281 g zucchini, shredded and squeezed of excess water
6.8 oz/192 g blackberries, plus more for garnish
Edible flowers, for garnish (optional)

HAZELNUT APRICOT CAKE WITH CHOCOLATE CHIPS

Makes one 10-inch cake

CAKE
7.6 oz/216 g sunflower oil
8.8 oz/250 g coconut sugar
1 lb/454 g milk
.4 oz/10 g vanilla extract
4.4 oz/125 g Greek yogurt
12.7 oz/360 g all-purpose flour
7.7 oz/219 g hazelnut flour
½ tsp/2 g baking soda
1¼ tsp/6 g baking powder
¼ tsp/1 g kosher salt
6.4 oz/182 g dark chocolate mini
    chocolate chips or finely chopped dark
    chocolate
7.1 oz/200 g dried apricot, chopped
Chamomile Cream (recipe follows)
Wildflower Simple Syrup (page 196)
Chamomile flowers, for garnish
Roses, for garnish

I chose coconut sugar for this recipe because traditional sugar cane production is an environmental strain. Coconut sugar requires less water, and the plants can be grown for up to 20 years, versus sugar cane that must be planted each year. The swap won't make your recipes taste like coconut, but they will account for a small change that makes a bigger impact.

1. Preheat the oven to 350°F/175°C. Butter and flour a 10-inch cake pan.
2. For the cake, in a large bowl, combine the oil, sugar, milk, vanilla, and yogurt in a bowl. Stir well to combine.
3. In a separate bowl, combine the flours, baking soda, baking powder, and salt. Mix to combine, then add to the bowl with the yogurt mixture. Mix to combine.
4. Fold in the chocolate and apricots.
5. Pour into the prepared cake pan, spreading to the edges with an offset spatula.
6. Bake until golden brown and a knife piercing the center comes out clean, about 40 minutes.
7. Remove from oven and let cool in the pan for about 10 minutes, then turn out onto a rack to cool fully.
8. To assemble, use a long serrated knife to slice the cooled cake in three even layers. Soak each layer with the wildflower syrup.
9. Place the first layer on a serving dish or cake board. Top with about one third of the chamomile cream and spread into an even layer.
10. Place the second layer. Top with about one third of the chamomile cream and spread into an even layer.
11. Place the final layer of cake and top with the remaining cream. Spread to the edges of the cake. Use an offset palate knife to smooth the exterior of the cake. It will not cover the entire cake.
12. Garnish the cake with chamomile flowers and roses.

CHAMOMILE CREAM

Makes enough for one 10-inch layer cake

1 lb 12.2 oz/800 g heavy cream
.7 oz/20 g fresh or dried chamomile
    flowers
2.3 oz/65 g honey
3.5 oz/100 g mascarpone cheese

1. In a heavy-bottomed saucepan, heat the cream to 140°F/60°C. Remove from the heat and add the chamomile flowers. Set aside to infuse for ten minutes.
2. Strain and set aside to cool.
3. In the bowl of a stand mixer fitted with the paddle attachment, combine the infused cream with the mascarpone and honey. Whip until thickened and smooth.

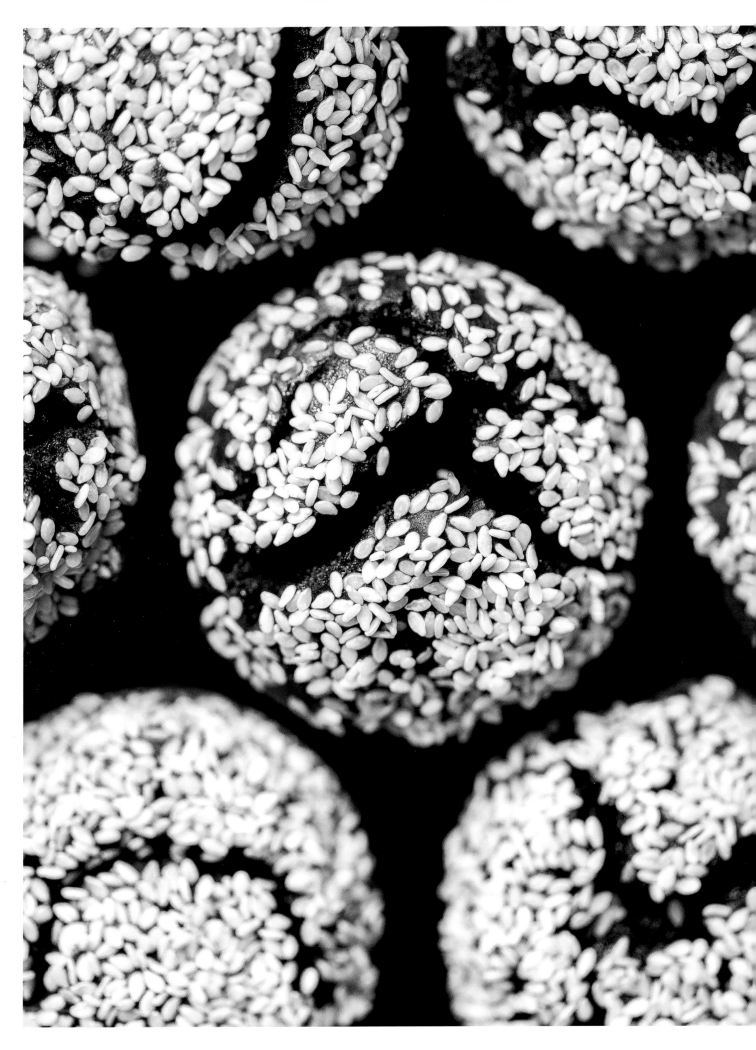

BLACK BEAN SESAME CAKES

Makes 12 cakes

Beans are sort of a magical ingredient. They're nutrient-dense and full of protein, but they also can provide structure and texture in place of many less nutritious ingredients. In this recipe, I used black beans in place of flour. There is no flavor of beans, making this a wonderful base recipe to personalize with additional flavors and inclusions, like nuts, dried fruit, or chopped chocolate.

15 oz canned black beans
1 oz/28 g coconut oil
5.3 oz/150 g eggs
.7 oz/20 g tahini
5.6 oz/160 g maple syrup
2.6 oz/75 g Dutch-processed cocoa powder
1 tsp/5 g baking powder
¼ tsp/2 g kosher salt
Sesame seeds, as needed for garnish

1. Preheat the oven to 350°F/175°C. Grease and flour a cupcake pan.
2. Place the black beans in a blender and blend for about 20 seconds. Add the oil, eggs, and tahini and blend for another 20 seconds.
3. Add the syrup, cocoa powder, baking powder, and salt, and blend until smooth.
4. Pour into the wells of the prepared cupcake pan and sprinkle with sesame seeds.
5. Bake until the center of the cakes spring back when touched, about 15 minutes.
6. Set aside to cool slightly before unmolding.

PEAR LENTIL MUFFINS

Makes 12 muffins

5 oz/142 g sugar

1 tsp/4 g kosher salt

2 oz/57 g eggs, room temperature

3.2 oz/90 g vegetable oil

6 oz/170 g whole milk

11 oz/312 g red lentil flour

2 tsp/10 g freshly grated nutmeg

.5 oz/13 g baking powder

3 oz/85 g chopped D'Anjou pear, skin on

In these muffins, we're using red lentil flour in place of the all-purpose flour. In addition to being a healthy addition to our diet, lentils require no added water to grow, so no irrigation is necessary for the crop, making them a sustainable and delicious ingredient. I like the sweet D'Anjou pears here, but you can use any variety that is local to you. You can also substitute your favorite apple.

1. Preheat a convection oven to 350°F/177°C.
2. Oil or line the wells of a standard muffin pan.
3. In large mixing bowl, combine the sugar, salt, eggs, oil, and milk. Whisk to combine. Sift the flour, nutmeg, and baking powder into the bowl, and mix until nearly combined.
4. Fold in the pears.
5. Scoop into the prepared pan. Transfer to the oven and bake until golden brown and the center bounces back when pressed lightly, about 22 minutes.
6. Transfer to a rack to cool.

DAIRY-FREE PUMPKIN TRAVEL CAKE

Makes one 9-inch loaf

This is a simple dairy-free pumpkin cake that uses oat milk as a substitute for whole milk. Of the milk alternatives, oat milk is one of the creamiest, making it a great substitute for rich, full-fat dairy. I used a fun bubble mold for my cake, but you can use any loaf or cake pan you'd like.

1. Preheat the oven to 350°F/175°C. Butter and flour a 9-inch loaf pan.
2. In the bowl of a stand mixer fitted with the paddle attachment, combine the sugar, salt, eggs, oil, milk, and pumpkin. Mix on medium-low until combined.
3. In a separate bowl, sift together the bread flour, cake flour, baking powder, nutmeg, and cinnamon. Add to the pumpkin mixture and mix until just combined.
4. Transfer to the prepared cake pan.
5. Bake until a knife inserted into the center of the cake comes out clean, about 40 minutes. Set on a rack to cool.
6. To make the glaze, whisk together the sugar and milk in a medium bowl.
7. Pour the glaze over the cooled cake and sprinkle with the oats and pumpkin seeds. Let set for at least 30 minutes before serving.

5 oz/142 g sugar
¾ tsp/4 g kosher salt
2 oz/57 g eggs, room temperature
3 oz/85 g vegetable oil
6 oz/170 g oat milk
3 oz/85 g pumpkin purée
5 oz/142 g bread flour
4 oz/113 g cake flour
2 tsp/13 g baking powder
3/4 tsp/3 g grated nutmeg
2 tsp/10 g ground cinnamon

GLAZE

4 oz/113 g confectioners' sugar
2 oz/57 g oat milk
Toasted oats, as needed for garnish
Toasted pumpkin seeds, as needed for garnish

CRICKET BROWNIES

Makes 30 brownies

4.4 oz/125 g semi-sweet chocolate
 (70%), roughly chopped
6 oz/171 g peanut butter
3.3 oz/94 g unsalted butter
5.6 oz/160 g eggs, room temperature
6.6 oz/188 g sugar
1.8 oz/50 g cocoa powder
1 ½ tbsp/10 g hemp flour
1.2 oz/35 g cricket flour

Some sweet tooths may not be ready for bugs in their desserts, but I'm going to introduce them to you anyway! Crickets have an outstanding amount of protein, and they are abundant and very sustainable—one of the most sustainable animal proteins and very popular in many parts of the world. If you're hesitant, there is not enough cricket flour in this recipe for the taste to come through much, so it's the perfect way to get your feet wet with a valuable ingredient.

1. Preheat the oven to 350°F/175°C. Butter a 9-by 13-in baking pan; set aside.
2. In a bowl over a hot water bath, melt the chocolate, peanut butter, and butter. Set aside.
3. In the bowl of a stand mixer fitted with the whisk attachment, whip the eggs and about half of the sugar until doubled in volume, about 4 minutes.
4. While whipping on low speed, add the melted butter mixture to the eggs. Mix to combine. Add the remaining sugar, cocoa powder, hemp flour, and cricket flour and mix just until combined.
5. Spread into the prepared sheet pan.
6. Bake until the center springs back when touched, about 15 minutes. Cool fully before slicing.

COCONUT MADELEINES

Makes about 100 pieces

Madeleines are a popular one – or two-bite cakes that are served with coffee or tea, or as part of a small bite dessert course. This version is dairy-free and made with coconut sugar for a nice, light flavor and texture. The recipe yields quite a few Madeleines, but they are a great gift and freeze well for later.

1. In a small bowl, combine the coconut oil and sorghum syrup. Warm lightly over a hot water bath; set aside. In a separate bowl, soft together the flour, baking powder, and salt; set aside.
2. In a clean bowl, whip the egg whites and coconut sugar until frothy and light in color.
3. Add the dry ingredients in three editions, mixing until combined between each addition.
4. Stream the coconut sorghum mixture into the batter, stirring just until combined.
5. Cover and refrigerate overnight.
6. Preheat the oven to 375°F/190°C.
7. Transfer the batter to a piping bag with no tip. Pipe into a greased Madeleine pan
8. Bake until golden brown, 5 to 7 minutes. The center will rise more than the edges.
9. Transfer to a cooling rack to cool.

1 lb/470 g coconut oil
2.2 oz/61 g sorghum syrup
1 lb 2.7 oz/529 g eggs
1 lb/449 g coconut sugar
1 lb 1 oz/476 g all-purpose flour
.6 oz/16 g baking powder
1 tsp/5 g kosher salt
Zest of 1 lime

TIGER NUT-FLOUR WAFFLE

Makes about 5 waffles, depending on size

3.5 oz/100 g eggs
.7 oz/21 g sugar
4 oz/114 g tiger nut milk
1.8 oz/50 grapeseed oil
.4 oz/10 g vanilla extract
4.2 oz/120 g tiger nut flour
.1 oz/3 g baking powder
¼ tsp/1 g kosher salt

You don't find a lot of tiger nut recipes today, but this earthy, slightly sweet nut is becoming increasingly popular. They are a drought-resistant crop that flourishes without pesticides or fertilizer and serves as a cover crop to help regenerate soil in between growing seasons. Choosing a more earth-friendly nut is a simple, small change for more mindful baking.

1. In a large bowl, stir together the eggs and sugar. Add the milk, oil, and vanilla, and stir to combine.
2. Add the flour, baking powder, and salt, and mix just until combined.
3. Spoon batter into a greased waffle pan and cook according to the manufacturer's directions.

FLAX SEED CRACKERS

Makes about 150 crackers, based on size and shape

Flax (along with hemp and chia seeds) are among the most sustainable plants we can consume. They contribute nutrients when added to smoothies, yogurt, or anything else you might sprinkle them on, but they also make an excellent plant-forward egg replacer. This cracker recipe is gluten-free, egg-free, and dairy-free, which means it can be a universal staple of any snack or cocktail spread.

10.6 oz/300 g flax meal
7.6 oz/215 g water
1½ tsp/7 g kosher salt
2 tsp/14 g Onion Powder (page 202)

1. Preheat the oven to 400°F/204°C.
2. In a large bowl, combine the flax, water, salt, and onion powder. Mix by hand until an even dough forms.
3. Spread evenly on a silicone-lined baking sheet until the mixture is about ⅛-inch thick. Gently cut into any shape you like, re-using scraps to make more crackers.
4. Bake until the crackers are crisp with golden brown edges, 15 to 20 minutes.
5. Cool fully. Store in an air-tight container until use.

DAIRY-FREE COCONUT CAKE DONUTS

Makes 1 dozen donuts

5.3 oz/150 g sugar
15 oz/425 g cake flour
3.4 oz/95 g bread flour
1½ tsp/8 g kosher salt
3 tsp/15 g baking powder
1.8 oz/50 g egg, room temperature
1.8 oz/50 g egg yolks, room temperature
15.9 oz/450 grams cream of coconut
2.6 oz/75 g coconut milk, room
  temperature
.9 oz/25 g vegetable oil
1½ tsp/6 g vanilla extract
Vegetable oil, as needed for frying
1 cup honey, for finishing
1½ cups coconut flakes, for finishing

A preference for non-dairy foods are at an increase, due to intolerances, health concerns, or environmental factors. Regardless of the reason, non-dairy sweets can be hard to come by, especially favorite classics like donuts. This cake donut recipe uses coconut and cream of coconut for a rich and tender donut that will stand-up to a traditional donut.

1. In a bowl, mix together the sugar, cake flour, bread flour, salt, and baking powder. Set aside.
2. In the bowl of a stand mixer fitted with a paddle attachment, combine the eggs, yolks, cream of coconut, coconut milk, oil, and vanilla extract.
3. Add the dry ingredients all at once and mix, scraping the bowl as needed, until homogenous, about 2 minutes.
4. Transfer the batter to a lightly oiled bowl. Cover and set aside to rest for 20 minutes.
5. Select a pot that is wider than it is deep. Fill it about halfway with oil and heat to 365°F/185°C. You can also use a deep fryer.
6. Use a donut dropper to deposit the batter into the hot oil (see note). Fry, turning as needed, until golden brown all over, about 1 minute per side. Remove with a wire spider and transfer to a rack set over a baking sheet to drain. Tear the first donut open to check the doneness and adjust the cooking time as needed for a fully cooked, fluffy interior.
7. Place the honey in a shallow bowl. Dip each cooled donut into the honey on one side only. Sprinkle with coconut flakes.

Note: Donut depositors are manual tools that you can find at most baking supply stores. If you do not have a depositor, you can drop the donuts with an approximately ½ cup scoop, but the cooking times will vary.

HEMP FLOUR WHOOPIE PIES WITH APPLE BUTTER AND CONCORD GRAPE JELLY

Makes about 25 cookie sandwiches

Hemp flour is very high in protein, containing more than beef, and it contains all nine of the essential amino acids, making it a complete protein. It is a highly sustainable and low-impact plant. It has a strong taste, and the cookie portion of this recipe is intensely flavored. Once it's paired with the jelly and apple butter, however, you are left with a slight earthiness that balances beautifully with the fruit.

19.4 oz/551 g hemp flour
19.4 oz/551 g confectioners' sugar
14.6 oz/414 g egg whites

6.9 oz/196 g egg whites
2.8 oz/78 g water
15.5 oz/440 g granulated sugar
Silken Apple Butter (recipe below)
Concord Grape Jelly (recipe below)

1. Preheat the oven to 350°F/175°C. Line two baking sheets with silicone baking mats.
2. In a large mixing bowl, combine the hemp flour and confectioners' sugar. Blend in the egg whites, and set aside.
3. In the bowl of a stand mixer fitted with a paddle attachment, whip the egg whites over medium speed. While they whip, combine the water and sugar in a small saucepan. Bring to a boil and without stirring, cook until it reaches 248°F/120°C.
4. Stream the hot syrup into the whipping egg whites. Increase the speed to medium-high and whip to stiff peaks, about 4 minutes.
5. Fold the reserved hemp flour mixture into the meringue. Transfer to a piping bag with a medium straight tip.
6. Pipe 2-inch circles onto the prepared baking sheets.
7. Bake until brown around the edges and the center springs back when pressed lightly, about 20 minutes. Remove from the oven and set aside to cool fully.
8. To assemble, match the cookies together to make pairs of similar shapes and sizes.
9. Lay half of the cookies flat-side up. Pipe a ring of apple butter around the outer rim of the cookie. Fill the center with apple butter. Top with its matching cookie.
10. Serve right away.

SILKEN APPLE BUTTER

Makes enough for 25 whoopie pies

12.3 oz/350 g Silken apples (or another apple, like Macintosh), roughly chopped including skin and core
1.3 oz/36 g brown sugar
¼ tsp/1 g kosher salt
1.6 oz/45 g unsalted butter

1. In a medium pot, combine the apples, sugar, salt, and butter. Bring to a boil.
2. Continue cooking over low to medium heat until the mixture thickens and darkens in color, about 1½ hours.
3. Remove from the heat and set aside to cool slightly. Carefully blend in countertop blender. Strain through a fine mesh sieve.
4. Cool before transferring to a covered container. Refrigerate until needed.

CONCORD GRAPE JELLY

Makes enough for 25 whoopie pies

10.6 oz/300 g concord grapes
1.1 oz/30 g granulated sugar

1. Over a mixing bowl, separate the skin from the flesh of the grapes. Reserve the skins in the bowl and the flesh in a heavy-bottomed saucepan.
2. Cook the grapes over medium-high heat until they begin to lose their shape, about 15 minutes. Strain to remove the pits, pushing through the strainer to capture all of the juice.
3. Return the strained liquid to the pot and add the reserved skins. Cook until the mixture has cooked down, about 45 minutes.
4. Transfer to a baking sheet to cool before transferring to a covered container. Refrigerate until needed.

Note: For a thicker jelly, add 1.1 oz/30 g of sugar and .4 oz/10g of pectin. Bring to a boil, then add 50 g lemon juice.

GRAPES

Technically, grapes are berries, but because they include so many varieties and have so many different uses, they are usually grouped separately. There are varieties of grapes, both with seeds and seedless.

Grapes vary greatly in color from pale green to deep purple. Choose grapes that are plump and juicy, with smooth skins that have a pale gray film (known as bloom). Grapes should be firmly attached to their green stems. There are varieties of grapes with skin that easily slips off the fruit (Concord), and other varieties in which the skin remains firmly intact (Thompson seedless).

Grapes from California will come into season in late May for some red grapes, and June or July for Thompson, and last into early December. Grapes in the eastern United States have a shorter season, becoming available in August and then gone by November.

VARIETY	DESCRIPTION
Thompson seedless	Medium size. Green, thin skin. Seedless. Sweet, mild flavor.
Concord	Blue-black, thick skin slips easily from flesh. Sweet flavor.
Black	Large. Deep purple skin. Usually with seeds. Very sweet flavor.
Red Emperor	Light to deep red, with green streaking; thin, tightly adhering skin. Sweet flavor. Usually with seeds
Champagne/ Black Corinth	1/4-inch diameter. Red to light purple. Seedless. Juicy and sweet.
Red flame	Hybrid of the Thompson grape. Seedless. Round in shape. Bright, medium-red color. Firm crunch and sweet flavor.
Ruby red	Seedless. Elongated shape. Juicy and sweet.
Red Globe	Seeded. Large and round. Low in acid. Fairly sweet.
Tokay	Seeded. Elongated. Bland flavor.
Reliance	Small. Pale red to golden in color. Very flavorful.
Black Beauty	Seedless. Small and oblong. Rich, dark color. Bright, sweet, spicy flavor.
Venus	Seedless. Large and round. Rich, dark color. Sweet flavor; astringent skin.

BLUE SPIRULINA OAT MINT TRUFFLES

Makes 200 truffles

I like using the blue spirulina not only for its color but for its flavor as well. To me, it tastes like when you walk into a lake and smell of the air around you. It adds a freshness of nature and a welcome umami, or savory, taste when you bite the truffle.

1. In a saucepan, bring the oat milk to a boil. Remove from the heat, add the milk, and blend using an immersion or countertop blender. Steep for 5 minutes, then strain through a fine mesh sieve.
2. Weigh the oat milk, and add more, as needed, to return to the original 14 oz/400 g weight.
3. Transfer to a clean pot and add the glucose syrup and salt. Bring to a boil.
4. Meanwhile, combine the chocolate and cocoa butter in a heat-safe bowl. Pour the boiling oat milk mixture over the chocolate. Use an immersion blender to blend until smooth. Set aside to cool too 90°F/32°C.
5. Transfer the mixture to a piping bag. Fill the truffle shells to the top edge. Set aside at room temperature (or the refrigerator for about 20 minutes) until the ganache is firm.
6. Using a piping bag or small metal spatula, cover the opening of the truffle with just enough tempered chocolate to cover the ganache. Set aside until the chocolate is set and firm.
7. Once set, roll the truffles in melted dark chocolate, then in blue spirulina to coat. Remove excess powder by gently tossing in a mesh sifter.

14 oz/400 g oat milk, plus more as needed
.7 oz/20 g black mint leaves
.9 oz/25 g glucose syrup
1 tsp/4 g kosher salt
11.5 oz/325 g 72% dark chocolate, finely chopped
1.9 oz/55 g cocoa butter
200 dark chocolate truffle shells

Melted and tempered dark chocolate, as needed for finishing
Blue spirulina, as needed or coating.

YACON COTTON CANDY

Makes about 8 servings

3 cups/710 mL yacon syrup

Yacon is a root vegetable grown only in Peru, with a resemblance to the sweet potato. Yacons are processed to produce a natural sweetener with one third the calories of sugar cane. It is typically used in syrup form, with a caramel-like flavor and dark color. This one-ingredient recipe is intended to show off the flavor of this underutilized ingredient.

1. Pour the syrup into a heavy-bottom pot over medium heat. Cook until the mixture reaches 310°F/155°C.
2. Pour onto a silicone-lined baking sheet and set aside to cool. It will harden completely.
3. Break up pieces of the hardened syrup and blend to a powder in a blender or food processor.
4. Use in a cotton candy machine according to manufacturer's directions.

VEGAN RED WINE QUINCE GUMMY FLOWERS

Makes about 25 pieces

These gummies get their texture from an algae called agar agar. A plant-based alternative to gelatin, it provides a different mouthfeel to gelatin with a slightly more brittle bite. Gelatin and agar agar have very different techniques, so this is a great introduction to the ingredient if you haven't tried it before.

1. In a blender, combine the quince and water. Blend to a smooth purée. Set aside.
2. In a small bowl, whisk together the sugar and agar agar.
3. Meanwhile, place the water in a medium saucepot. While whisking, stream the sugar mixture into the water. Bring the water to a boil and add the glucose syrup. Continue to cook until the temperature on a thermometer reads 223°F/106°C.
4. Remove from the heat and add the reserved purée. Whisk until homogenous.
5. Pipe the mixture into any candy mold and set aside to set fully, at least an hour. Unmold and toss in sugar before serving.

5 oz/142 g Red Wine-Poached Quince and 3 oz/85 g poaching liquid (page 110)

.2 oz/6 g agar agar

5.3 oz/151 g cold water

6.6 oz/186 g granulated sugar

5.5 oz/157 g glucose syrup

Granulated sugar, as needed for finishing

MAPLE PEANUT BRITTLE

Makes two 13 – by 18-inch slabs

10 oz/283 g maple sugar
4 oz/113 g unsalted butter
Water, as needed
1½ tsp/7 g baking soda
.5 oz/14 g kosher salt
8 oz/227 g whole roasted peanuts

Maple syrup, the sap of the maple tree, is one of the more flavorful sweeteners, and maple sugar retains the caramel-like flavor of the syrup in a more familiar format for baking and candy-making. Be sure you're using real maple syrup or maple sugar. Always check your sources and ingredients.

1. In a heavy-bottomed saucepan, combine the sugar and butter. Add enough water to moisten the sugar to the appearance of wet sand. Bring to a boil over medium-high heat.
2. Cook, swirling the pan occasionally for even cooking, until the mixture is bubbling and medium-golden brown, about 8 minutes.
3. Remove from the heat and add the baking soda and salt. The mixture will bubble up, but then recede slightly. Add the peanuts and fold in gently to combine.
4. Place two silicone baking mats on a heat-safe surface. Divide the mixture between the two mats. Place a third silicone mat or a well-oiled piece of parchment paper over the first slab of brittle. Use a rolling pin to roll the mat and flatten the brittle. Transfer the top mat to the other slab and repeat.
5. When the brittle is completely cooled, break it into pieces. Store in an air-tight container.

MAPLE CARAMEL APPLES

Makes 10 servings

There are thousands of apple varieties, and I especially like to use antique, or heirloom, varieties for this recipe. Some of my favorites in my region are Blue Pearmain, Cameo, Chenango Strawberry, and Silken, but seek out the ones you like best where you are. This recipe uses maple syrup and sugar, since it is more environmentally friendly than cane sugar, but also adds an extra layer of caramel flavor to the candy crunch. I've used rose stems, since apples are botanically a member of the rose family, but you can use traditional candy sticks if you prefer.

10 small apples, washed and dried
14.1 oz/400 g maple sugar
7.1 oz/200 g maple syrup
5 oz/140 g apple cider
10 rose stems or candy sticks

1. Line a baking sheet with a silicone baking mat. Set aside.
2. In a saucepan over high heat, whisk together the maple sugar, syrup, and cider. Bring to a boil and continue cooking, without stirring, until it reaches 260° to 265°F/127° to 129°C. Remove from the heat.
3. On a heat-safe surface, place the saucepan with the maple caramel. Use a folded towel or other item to carefully prop one side of the saucepan so that it tilts, making a well of candy coating deep enough to coat the apples.
4. Working one at a time, carefully dip each apple into the maple candy, swirling to coat them entirely. Let excess drip into the pan, then transfer the apples to the prepared baking sheet.
5. Insert the rose stems or candy sticks, then set the apples aside to cool until the candy shell hardens completely, about 5 minutes. Serve right away or store in a tightly sealed container for no more than a day.

DATE, PEAR, AND FIG ICE POPS

Makes about 12 popsicles, depending on size

Date syrup is very sweet and filled with vitamins and nutrients. Dates themselves are a drought-resistant crop that need practically no water to thrive. To me, this makes them an obvious substitute for granulated cane sugar, especially considering their subtle caramel flavor that makes any recipe a little bit more complex and deeper in flavor.

6.3 oz/178 g cubed pear
2.6 oz/75 g water, plus more as needed
1½ tsp/10 g date syrup, plus more as needed
1.8 oz/50 g black mission figs, sliced

1. In a blender, combine the pear, water, and date syrup. Blend to a smooth purée.
2. Pour the mixture into popsicle molds, leaving some room at the top to accommodate the figs. Press figs into the popsicles, pressing against the sides of the mold.
3. Transfer to the freezer and freeze overnight.
4. Unmold to serve.

BLACK SESAME MACARONS WITH MILK CHOCOLATE CARAMEL CRÉMEUX

Makes about 50 macarons

1 lb 3.4 oz/551 g black sesame flour
1 lb 3.4 oz/551 g confectioners' sugar
6.4 oz/182 g egg whites (first)
6.9 oz/196 g egg whites (second)
15.5 oz/440 g granulated sugar
2.8oz/78 g water
Milk Chocolate Caramel Crémeux
 (recipe below)

Sesame is a wonderful, unique flavor for pastries. Even better, it is considered a superfood, and a sustainable one at that. Sesame plants are drought resistant and need little to no water or fertilizers to grow. Sesame and its flour can be found either white or black. I like using black sesame for its color, especially here where it makes the finished macaron look like a natural stone.

1. Preheat the oven to 350°F/177°C. Line two baking sheets with silicone baking mats.
2. Sift the flour and confectioners' sugar into a large bowl. Add the first egg whites and mix until combined. Set aside.
3. In the bowl of a stand mixer fitted with the whip attachment, whip the second egg whites on medium speed while you prepare the sugar solution.
4. In a saucepan, combine the sugar and water. Cook over moderate heat until the mixture reaches 248°F/120°C.
5. Slowly stream the hot sugar mixture into the whipping egg whites. Continue to whip until stiff peaks form.
6. Fold the sesame flour mixture into the whipped egg whites. Continue mixing until the proper consistency is reached: take a spoonful of batter and hold it over the bowl. Slowly pour it back into the bowl so it forms a ribbon falling off the spoon. Count to five, and if the ribbon settles back into the bowl by 5, stop stirring. If the mixture is still stiff, keep stirring until it is ready.
7. Transfer to a piping bag fit with a medium round (806) tip. Pipe the batter onto the prepared baking sheets into quarter-sized circles.
8. Set aside at room temperature until the macarons form a light skin over the surface, about an hour.
9. Transfer to the oven and bake until the macarons are firm and matte on top, about 12 minutes. When you try to pick one up from the pan, it should come off clean. Set aside to cool fully.
10. Line up the macarons and select pairs that match in size and shape. Pipe the cremeaux in the center of half the macarons and top with its pair. Gently press down to spread the filling.
11. Transfer the finished macarons to a baking sheet and wrap tightly. Freeze for at least 2 days to improve the texture. Freeze until ready to serve. Remove 2 hours before serving to defrost in the refrigerator.

MILK CHOCOLATE CARAMEL CRÉMEUX

Makes enough to fill 50 macarons

.1 oz/3 g gelatin sheets
2.7 oz/77 g egg yolks
9 oz/255 g heavy cream
11.3 oz/319 g milk
3.3 oz/94 g sugar
7.2 oz/204 g chopped milk chocolate
1.7 oz/49 g cacao paste

1. In a bowl, cover the gelatin with ice water. Set aside for at least 5 minutes until softened.
2. Place the egg yolks in a medium heat-safe bowl; set aside.
3. Meanwhile, in a heavy bottomed pot, bring the cream, milk, and sugar to a boil. Whisking constantly, pour about 1/3 of the milk mixture into the egg yolks. Pour the mixture back into the pot, whisking constantly until combined.
4. Place the chocolate and cacao paste in the same bowl used for the eggs. Pour the hot milk mixture over the chocolate. Let rest for a few minutes, then stir gently to emulsify. Strain through a sieve into a covered container. Refrigerate overnight.
5. Transfer the crémeux to a piping bag fitted with a round tip (805).

STAGES OF MERINGUE: SOFT, MEDIUM, AND STIFF PEAKS

Each of the various stages of meringue—soft, medium, and stiff peak—is best suited for specific applications.

A soft-peak meringue will cling to the whip when lifted but will not form a pointed peak. Soft-peak meringue is commonly used in soufflés.

With medium-peak meringue, a peak will form when the whip is lifted from the meringue but will droop slightly. Medium-peak meringue is used to lighten mixtures such as creams and batters.

When the whip is lifted from a stiff-peak meringue, a sharp point will form and remain in the meringue. Stiff-peak meringue is the best choice for piping and décor work, as it holds its shape.

All meringues should be glossy and smooth. If a stiff-peak meringue appears dry, dull, or lumpy, it has been overwhipped and will be difficult to work with.

Summer

Fall

Spring

Winter

Chapter 3: Seasonality

ONE OF THE MOST FUNDAMENTAL food rules that will never steer you wrong is this: fruits and vegetables grown close to your kitchen and picked at the peak of their growing season will taste best. With every day that passes and every mile an ingredient travels, you will experience some loss in flavor or texture that cannot be replaced, even by the most skilled chef. This is particularly true of baking and pastry, where fruit is often the focus of a dish, making the quality of the ingredient that much more important.

Of course, seasonality is not unform. You can pick juicy ripe strawberries in Florida while New York is still covered in snow, berries still months away. So, the partner to seasonality is locality. Buying local means a lot of things to different people, but to me, local is within miles of my home whenever possible. I live in the Hudson Valley, and I source as many ingredients as possible from local farmers' markets, trees growing in friends' backyards (and my own!), and yes, on the side of the road. This food is as fresh as it can be, grown minutes from my home, and, as an added benefit, generally less expensive than what you can find at a grocery store. Especially when it's free!

Eating seasonally and locally doesn't mean only eating tomatoes in the heart of summer. What a sad life to wait 10 months for a tomato salad! Fruits and vegetables of all kinds are suited to freezing, drying, or preserving in other ways, like canning. Many farms or community centers offer classes in at-home preserving and can be a great resource for learning the best way to keep your ingredients.

Whether in a professional bakeshop or your own home kitchen, you will benefit from learning as much as possible about your community and the food grown within it. Meander slowly through farmers' markets, take long walks, paying attention to the trees and bushes around you. And don't forget to ask friends and colleagues where *they* find their produce and other ingredients, because you are sure to unearth a hidden gem.

ACORN SABLE COOKIES

Makes about 3 dozen cookies, depending on size

Acorns were once a high-fiber staple of the human diet, abundant throughout the Hudson Valley and beyond. Today, they are mostly left to the squirrels to enjoy— but we are reclaiming the acorn in this buttery sable cookie, rich in color thanks to acorn starch and flour. I've shaped them as pinecones as an homage to the acorn-keepers, but you can use any shape cutter you like, or even just as hand-cut squares or rectangles. You can find both acorn starch and flour at specialty stores or online markets, but you can also make your own flour from foraged acorns.

3.4 oz/95 g acorn starch
8.8 oz/250 g all-purpose flour
5.3 oz/150 g acorn flour
11.3 oz/319 g unsalted butter, soft
7.1 oz/200 g confectioners' sugar
4.2 oz/118 g eggs
3/4 tsp/3 g kosher salt

1. Into a bowl, sift together the acorn starch, all-purpose flour, and acorn flour.
2. In a mixer fitted with the paddle attachment, cream the butter and sugar until smooth and incorporated.
3. Add about 3 tablespoons/45 mL of the dry ingredients and mix to combine.
4. Add the eggs in two additions, mixing until fully incorporated between each addition. Scrape the bowl as needed.
5. Add the remaining dry ingredients and mix until just combined.
6. Refrigerate the dough for at least 30 minutes or up to overnight.
7. Cut the cookies to your desired shape and transfer to a silicone-lined baking sheet. Refrigerate for at least 10 minutes.
8. Preheat a convection oven to 325°F/160°C. For a conventional oven, preheat to 350°F/176°C.
9. Bake until the cookies are firm around the edges and matte on top, 12 to 15 minutes.

PUMPKIN-MAPLE SUGAR COOKIE WITH POMEGRANATE ICING

Makes 24 cookies

5.5 oz/155 g unsalted butter
12.1 oz/342 g maple sugar
2 oz/57 g eggs
3.5 oz/100 g pumpkin purée
.5 oz/14 g honey
15 oz/425 g all-purpose flour
½ tsp/2 g baking soda
¾ tsp/4 g kosher salt
1½ tsp/10 g freshly grated nutmeg
1 tsp/5 g ground cinnamon
2.1 oz/60 g pomegranate juice
10.8 oz/305 g confectioners' sugar
Pomegranate seeds, as needed for
  garnish

To prepare fresh pumpkin purée, quarter a sugar pumpkin and remove the seeds. Roast in a 400°F oven until tender, about 60 minutes. Scoop out the pulp and blend. Reserve any unused purée in the freezer.

The Hudson Valley is known for its produce and farms, and some favorite fall activities are pumpkin and apple picking. But at the same time, there are pomegranates growing all over the area with few of us even knowing they are available to pick! Pomegranate and pumpkin together is a beautiful flavor combination, and the pomegranate gives the icing a natural shade of pink for a cute finish.

1. Preheat a convection oven to 325°F/160°C. For a non-convection oven, preheat to 350°F/175°C.
2. In the bowl of a stand mixer fitted with the paddle attachment, cream the butter and sugar until light and fluffy, about 4 minutes.
3. Add the eggs, pumpkin, and honey in four additions, mixing between each addition and scraping the bowl as needed.
4. In a medium bowl, sift together the flour, baking soda, salt, nutmeg, and cinnamon. Add to the mixing bowl all at once and mix on low speed until combined.
5. Use a 2 oz (¼ cup) scoop to scoop the cookies onto a baking sheet.
6. Bake until the cookies are golden around the edges, about 15 minutes.
7. Transfer to a rack to cool completely.
8. Meanwhile, combine the pomegranate juice and confectioners' sugar in a bowl and mix until smooth.
9. Dip the cooled cookies in icing and top with pomegranate seeds. Set aside for at least 2 hours for the icing to harden.

PINECONE SABLES

Makes 24 cookies, depending on shape

The Hudson Valley is bursting with pinecones, and inside those pinecones are pinenuts—a delicious, tiny little nut that is tedious to retrieve, but worth the effort! If you don't have access to foraged pinecones, you can use purchased pinenuts.

1. In the bowl of a stand mixer fitted with the paddle attachment, cream the butter and sugar until well incorporated.
2. Add about 2 tablespoons of the flour and mix to combine.
3. Add the eggs in two parts, mixing well between each addition and scraping as needed.
4. Add the remaining flour, corn starch, and ground pinenuts. Mix just until incorporated.
5. Cover and set aside to rest for at least 30 minutes or up to overnight.
6. On a floured surface, roll the dough to about ¼-in/6-mm. Use a cookie cutter to cut out cookies, transfer to a silicone-line baking sheet, and refrigerate for 10 minutes.
7. Preheat the oven to 325°F/160°C. Bake until firm and matte on top, about 15 minutes. Transfer to a rack to cool.

11.3 oz/319g unsalted butter, soft
7.1 oz/200g confectioners' sugar
8.8 oz/250g all-purpose flour
3.6 oz/95g corn starch
5.3 oz/150g pinenuts, finely ground
4.2 oz/118g eggs
1 tsp/3g

RED SHISO CAKE

Makes one 6-inch layer cake

Bittersweet Flourless Chocolate Cake
  (recipe below)
Wildflower Simple Syrup (page 196)
Vanilla Buttercream (page 202)
Shiso Diplomat Cream (recipe below)
Fresh red shiso leaves, for garnish
Chocolate shiso leaves (optional), for
  garnish

Shiso is an aromatic herb that grows beautifully in the Hudson Valley. Part of the mint family, shiso is heart-shaped with saw-toothed edges, with a bright herbaceous flavor. There are several varieties of shiso, but I've chosen the red leaves for this recipe, to add a bit of a spicier and floral flavor. For garnish, I've brushed the shiso leaves themselves with melted chocolate to create chocolate leaves—using nature as the best pastry tool. You can use this technique with any edible leaf for a realistic shape that shows all the details.

1. Place one cake layer on a cake board or serving plate. Use a pastry brush to brush with simple syrup to lightly soak the cake.
2. Place the buttercream in a piping bag with a medium-sized round tip. Pipe a ring of buttercream around the edge of the cake layer to make a border, then fill the ring with the diplomat cream, smoothing the top with a spatula.
3. Place a second layer of cake and repeat by brushing with simple syrup, piping the buttercream, and adding the diplomat cream. Repeat again, finishing with a layer of cake.
4. Pipe the remaining buttercream around the sides and top of the cake, and smooth with an offset metal spatula. Garnish with shiso leaves and chocolate, as desired.

BITTERSWEET FLOURLESS CHOCOLATE CAKE

Makes enough for one 6-inch layer cake

9.3 oz/265 g egg yolks
11.5 oz/327 g sugar, divided use
2.5 oz/70 g cocoa powder
9.2 oz/260 g egg whites

1. Preheat the oven to 350°F/175°C.
2. In a mixer fitted with the whip attachment, beat the egg yolks with half of the sugar. White until the mixture is very light in color and falls from the whip like a ribbon, about 3 minutes. Transfer to a large bowl.
3. Gently fold in the cocoa powder.
4. Add the egg whites to a clean mixing bowl fitted with the whip. Whip on medium speed and slowly add the remaining sugar. Whip until the egg whites form a stiff meringue, about 5 minutes.
5. Fold the yolk mixture into the egg whites until combined.
6. Spread on two 13-in by 9-in/33-cm by 23-cm parchment paper-lined baking sheets.
7. Bake until the cake springs back and a toothpick inserted into the center comes out clean, 10 to 15 minutes.
8. Set aside to cool fully.
9. Once cool, cut out two 6-inch/15-cm rings from each pan, for four total.

SHISO DIPLOMAT CREAM

Makes enough for one 6-inch layer cake

1 lb 1.6 oz/500 g milk, plus as needed
1.6 oz/45 g red shiso leaves
1.8 oz/50 g pastry cream powder
4.4 oz/125 g sugar
4.2 oz/120 g egg yolks
½ tsp/2 g kosher salt
1.8 oz/50 g unsalted butter
1½ silver gelatin sheets
1 lb 1.6 oz/500 g heavy cream, whipped
    to soft peaks

1. In a saucepan over medium heat, bring the milk to 140°F/60°C. Remove from the heat, add the shiso leaves, and set aside to steep for 10 minutes. Strain. Measure the milk and add additional milk as needed to return to 500 g/1 lb 1.6 oz and return to the saucepan.
2. In a bowl, whisk together the pastry cream powder and sugar to remove any lumps. Add the egg yolks and whisk until smooth to form a liaison. Set aside.
3. Return the milk to the stove and bring to a boil over medium heat. Whisk a small amount of the boiling milk into the egg mixture, then slowly whisk the egg mixture into the saucepan of milk.
4. Bring to a boil, whisking constantly to avoid lumps, until the mixture is thickened and smooth.
5. Immediately transfer the mixture to the bowl of a stand mixer fitted with the paddle attachment and add the butter. Mix at medium speed until the cream has cooled to room temperature.
6. Once cool, fold in the whipped cream until smooth.

USING GELATIN

Gelatin is used as a stabilizer in many bakeshop preparations. In small amounts, gelatin adds body; in greater amounts, it can set a liquid so firmly that it can be sliced or cut into shapes. Using the precise amount of gelatin is crucial: If too little is used, it will not add enough stabilizing power, while if too much is used, the texture will become rubbery and unpalatable, and the flavor undesirable.

Gelatin is a protein composed of molecules that attract water; gelatin is hydrated, or bloomed, in order to allow these molecules to swell, absorbing moisture.

1. Gelatin must be rehydrated, or bloomed, and then melted before use. To bloom, soak it in the amount of liquid specified in the formula, which should be approximately 8 oz/230 g of a water-based liquid for every 1 oz/28 g of granulated gelatin. An alternate method commonly used for blooming sheet gelatin is to soak the sheets in enough cold water to completely submerge them. If this method is used, after blooming gently squeeze and wring the sheets to force the excess water out, so as not to add additional liquid to the formula, which would change the consistency and flavor of the finished product.

2. After it is bloomed (hydrated), the gelatin must be melted. To melt bloomed gelatin, place it in a pan or bowl over low heat or a hot water bath until liquefied. Then stir the melted gelatin into a warm or room-temperature base mixture. (If the base is cold, the gelatin may set up prematurely.) If the base is quite warm or hot (at least 105°F/41°C), however, you may opt to add the bloomed gelatin directly to the hot base, rather than melting it separately, and allow the base's heat to melt the gelatin. Be sure to stir gelatin added this way until it is completely blended into the base.

As the bloomed gelatin is heated, the water-attracting molecules dissolve completely. Through cooling, the proteins in the gelatin mixture join together to form a three-dimensional web that holds the absorbed moisture. It is the development of this system in the gelatin that results in what we know as a gel; when added to other mixtures, or bases, the presence of this protein web is what results in a set, stabilized product.

APRICOT LEMON VERBENA PINK PEPPERCORN UPSIDE DOWN CAKE

Makes one 8-inch cake

Apricots are more commonly eaten dried rather than fresh, but a ripe fresh apricot is truly something special. They grow in abundance here in the Hudson Valley—I forage mine from a tree I planted in my yard! They are a hidden gem. The combination of apricot and lemon verbena is bright and floral, just like the pink peppercorns.

1. Preheat the oven to 325°F/160°C.
2. For the topping: in a bowl, combine the butter, peppercorns, and sugar. Smear the mixture in an even layer on the bottom of an 8-inch tube pan. Arrange the apricots flesh-side down in the mixture and set aside.
3. For the cake, bring the milk to a simmer in a saucepan over moderate heat. Remove from the heat and add the lemon verbena. Steep for 5 minutes, then strain and set aside to cool.
4. In the bowl of a mixer fitted with the paddle attachment, cream the butter and sugar until smooth. Add the eggs and vanilla in three additions, scraping the bowl as needed.
5. Combine the flour, salt, and baking powder in a small bowl. Add in three additions, alternating with the reserved milk. Mix well and scrape the bowl between each addition.
6. Spread the batter in the pan over the apricots.
7. Bake until golden brown, and the middle springs back when pressed, about 35 minutes.
8. Cool in the pan for about 15 minutes, then run a knife along the outside edge of the cake. Unmold onto a serving plate or cake circle. Serve warm, if possible.

TOPPING

4.1 oz/115g unsalted butter, melted

7.5 oz/212 g dark brown sugar

.7 oz/20g pink peppercorns, cracked, plus more for garnish

4 apricots, halved and pitted, plus more for garnish

CAKE

8 oz/226 g whole milk

1 tsp/10 g lemon verbena, plus more for garnish

3 oz/86 g unsalted butter

10.6 oz/300 g dark brown sugar

2 eggs

2 tsp/20g vanilla extract

10.6 oz/300 g all-purpose flour

1¼ tsp/6 g kosher salt

2½ tsp/20 g baking powder

STRAWBERRY SHORTCAKE

Makes one 8-inch layer cake

White Cake (recipe below)
Simple Syrup (page 196), as needed
Chantilly Cream (recipe below)
Strawberry Filling (recipe below)
Poached Snap Peas (recipe below)
Strawberries, for garnish
Pea tendrils, for garnish

Strawberries and peas have the same growing season, and they taste amazing together—so much so that I'm shocked it's not a more common duo. While you could use sugar in the strawberry filling, I prefer the floral flavors from a bit of honeydew melon purée when it's available.

1. Slice the cooled cake horizontally into three layers. Brush each layer with simple syrup.
2. Place the first layer on a cake circle or plate. Using a piping bag, pipe the Chantilly cream around the outer edge of the layer to create a border.
3. Place half of the strawberry filling in the center of the cake, sprinkle with half the peas, and cover with additional Chantilly.
4. Repeat with the second layer, reserving a few poached snap peas for garnish, and finish with the third layer of cake on top.
5. Frost the outside of the cake with the remaining Chantilly cream, and garnish with strawberries, reserved snap peas, and pea tendrils as desired.

WHITE CAKE

Makes one 8-inch cake

2.8 oz/80 g milk
2.1 oz/60 g eggs
1.6 oz/46 g egg yolks
6.6 oz/187 g sugar
6.3 oz/178 g Chiffon Flour (page 192)
.2 oz/6 g baking powder
½ tsp/4 g sea salt
.4 oz/10 g vanilla powder
3.7 oz/106 g unsalted butter, soft

1. Preheat the oven to 350°F.
2. In a medium bowl, combine the milk, eggs, and yolks. Set aside.
3. In the bowl of a stand mixer fitted with the paddle attachment, combine the sugar, flour, baking powder, salt, and vanilla powder. Add the soft butter and mix until light, fluffy, and homogenous.
4. Add half of the milk mixture and mix on low speed for 4 minutes. Scrape the bowl and add 1/3 of the remaining milk mixture, and mix on low for an additional 2 minutes.
5. Add another 1/3 of the milk mixture and mix on low speed for 2 minutes. Scrape the bowl, then add the remaining liquids and mix for a final 2 minutes.
6. Transfer to a greased 8-inch cake pan and bake until the cake is golden on top and springs back when touched, 20 to 30 minutes. Set on a rack to cool for 10 minutes before unmolding and cooling fully.

CHANTILLY CREAM

Makes enough for one 8-inch layer cake

1 lb 5.2 oz/600 g heavy cream
2.1 oz/60 g sugar

1. In the bowl of a stand mixer fitted with the whip attachment, whip the cream and sugar until soft to medium peaks form. Refrigerate until ready to use.

STRAWBERRY FILLING

Makes enough for one 8-inch layer cake

8.8 oz/250 g strawberries, roughly chopped
1 vanilla bean, scraped
.7 oz/20 g honeydew , blended to a purée

1. In a bowl, combine the strawberries, vanilla bean, and honeydew purée. Set aside for 20 minutes to macerate before using right away.

POACHED SNAP PEAS

Makes enough for one 8-inch layer cake

8.8 oz/200 g water
1.8 oz/50 g sugar
1.1 oz/30 g kosher salt
.9 oz/25 g snap peas

1. In a saucepan over medium heat, bring the water, sugar, and salt to a boil.
2. Add the peas and let cook until they turn bright green, about 1 minute. Remove with a slotted spoon and transfer to an ice bath to cool fully.

WHY SHOULD YOU USE MORE EDIBLE FLOWERS?

Nutritional Value: Some edible flowers are rich in vitamins, minerals, and antioxidants. For example, nasturtiums contain vitamin C and beta-carotene, while marigolds have antioxidant properties. Consuming a variety of flowers can diversify your nutrient intake.

Culinary Creativity: Edible flowers can add unique flavors, aromas, and colors to dishes, enhancing the overall dining experience. They can be used in salads, soups, desserts, and even as garnishes, allowing for creative culinary expression.

Aesthetic Appeal: Edible flowers can make dishes more visually appealing. Their vibrant colors and delicate shapes can turn an ordinary meal into a feast for the eyes, making them popular in fine dining and gourmet cuisine.

Cultural Significance: Many cultures have a tradition of incorporating flowers into their cuisine. For example, in Thai cuisine, flowers like orchids and jasmine are used to infuse fragrances and flavors into dishes and teas.

Sustainable Eating: Some edible flowers, such as nasturtiums and pansies, are easy to grow at home or in community gardens. Growing your own flowers for consumption can be a sustainable and environmentally friendly practice, reducing the need for commercial agriculture.

Connection to Nature: Consuming edible flowers can deepen your connection to nature and the seasons. It encourages people to explore their surroundings and learn about the plants and flowers in their region.

Potential Health Benefits: Some flowers, like hibiscus, are believed to have potential health benefits. Hibiscus tea, for instance, is thought to have heart-healthy properties and can help lower blood pressure.

Allergen-Free Options: For individuals with dietary restrictions or allergies, edible flowers can provide a unique and allergen-free way to add variety to their meals.

FIG AND PUMPKIN RICOTTA CHEESECAKE

Makes one 9-inch cake

Figs use very few resources and give back to the environment they are grown in, making them one of the most sustainable fruits. That's why I've piled this cheesecake high with sweet, fresh figs for a perfect autumn dessert.

1. Preheat the oven to 325°F/160°C.
2. To the bowl of a stand mixer fitted with the paddle attachment, add the sugar and then the impastata. Blend the ingredients in low speed for about 10 seconds. Scrape the bowl and paddle, and blend again for about 10 more seconds. Repeat a few more times to ensure there are no lumps.
3. In a small bowl, combine the eggs and yolk. Add gradually to the mixing bowl, a quarter at a time, scraping the bowl and paddle after each addition.
4. Add the cream, lemon and orange juice, and vanilla. Mix to incorporate, scraping down once more to ensure there are no lumps.
5. Oil a 9-inch cake pan and line with a silicone or parchment-paper circle. Fill the pan with the cheesecake batter. Place the cake pan in a shallow baking dish and transfer to the oven.
6. Use a pitcher to carefully pour enough water into the baking dish to come about halfway up the sides of the cake pan.
7. Bake until the cake is set, but the center still jiggles like gelatin. Remove from the oven and set aside to cool fully.
8. Unmold onto a serving plate and top with the figs, toasted pumpkin seeds, and candied pumpkin peel.

12 oz/340 g sugar
2 lb 8 oz/1.1 kg sheep impastata ricotta
10 oz/283 g eggs
1 oz/28 g egg yolk
5 oz/142 g heavy cream
Juice from ½ a lemon
Juice from ½ an orange
.5 oz/14 g vanilla extract
10 figs, halved, for garnish
½ cup/60 g roasted pumpkin seeds
Candied Pumpkin Peel (recipe below), for garnish

CANDIED PUMPKIN PEEL

Makes enough for one cake

1. In a medium saucepot, combine the water and sugar, and bring to a boil over moderate heat.
2. Add the pumpkin peel and reduce to a low simmer.
3. Simmer until the peel is tender and translucent, about 45 minutes.
4. Cool in the syrup until ready to use.

8.8 oz/250 g water
14 oz/400 g sugar
4.4 oz/250 g pumpkin peel, peeled with a knife or vegetable peeler

RED WINE-POACHED QUINCE "TART" WITH MEXICAN MARIGOLD MINT CRÉMEUX

Makes 15 servings

POACHED QUINCE
1 lb 1.6 oz/500 g red wine
3.5 oz/100 g maple syrup
1 quince, melon-balled

MEXICAN MARIGOLD MINT CRÉMEUX
.2 oz/6 g gelatin sheets
9.4 oz/267 g milk
9.4 oz/267g cream
.2 oz/5 g Mexican marigold mint
2.8 oz/80 g sugar
4.5 oz/128 g egg yolks
1 lb/454 g tempered dark chocolate
¼ cup/35 g toasted pine nuts
Mexican marigold mint, for garnish
Honeycomb, for garnish (optional)

I love quince, and this recipe brings it off the cheese board. Not an ideal fruit to eat out of hand, quince flesh is very hard and needs to be cooked to enjoy. I've poached in red wine here, giving it a beautiful color and tender bite, and paired it with one of my favorite herbs, Mexican marigold, for a very slight anise flavor. If you have any leftover quince, don't discard it! Cook it down until it forms a jelly.

1. For the quince: In a medium saucepan, bring the wine and maple syrup to a boil. Add the quince and reduce to a simmer. Cut a parchment circle to fit into the pan. Place inside the pot to cover the quince.
2. Simmer until the quince is tender and a knife pierced the flesh easily, about 15 minutes. Set aside to cool fully.
3. For the crémeux: hydrate the gelatin in a small bowl of ice water. Set aside.
4. In a medium saucepan over medium heat, bring the milk to a light simmer. Remove from the heat, add the mint, and set aside to steep for 8 minutes.
5. Meanwhile, combine about 1/3 of the sugar and the egg yolks in a heat-safe bowl.
6. Strain the mint from the milk. Re-measure and add enough milk to return to the original weight. Return to the pot and add the cream and remaining sugar.
7. Bring the milk mixture to a boil. Remove from the heat and pour about 1/4 of the milk mixture into the egg mixture, whisking constantly to temper.
8. Pour the tempered eggs and milk back into the saucepan, whisking constantly. Use a wooden spoon to stir constantly until the sauce coats the back of the spoon, about 5 minutes. Remove from the heat.
9. Strain the gelatin, squeezing out any excess water, and add to the hot sauce. Strain once more through a fine mesh sieve. Set aside to cool fully, then transfer to a pastry bag.
10. Spray a baking sheet with oil, then top with parchment paper.
11. Pour the tempered chocolate on the prepared baking sheet. Top with another piece of parchment and an inverted baking sheet, so that the top baking sheet is pressing the chocolate. After about 10 seconds, remove the top baking sheet and allow the chocolate to set. Remove the parchment and use a warm paring knife to cut a 4.5-in circle from the chocolate sheet.
12. Top the chocolate with quince and dots of crémeux. Sprinkle with the pine nuts, and garnish with the mint and honeycomb, if using.

CHESTNUT TART WITH TURBAN SQUASH DIPLOMAT CREAM

Makes one 12-inch by 5-inch tart

Turban Squash Diplomat Cream (recipe below)
Chestnut Confit (recipe below)
Chestnut Sable (recipe below)
Bourbon Whiskey Caramel (page 202)
Edible flowers, like nasturtium or sunflowers, for garnish (optional)

While chestnuts grow wild in many places, including the Hudson Valley, you may also have commercial chestnut farms where you can go pick your own. Be sure to bring thick gloves when foraging, as chestnuts have very thick, sharp spikes. The nuts grow in the same season as the lesser-known but just-as-sweet turban squash and lots of edible flowers, and as the saying goes, "What grows together goes together."

1. Pipe and spread about ¾ of the squash cream into the cooled tart shell.
2. Strain the chestnuts from the poaching liquid and arrange over the cream.
3. Pipe the remaining cream over the chestnuts, as desired. Drizzle with bourbon caramel and garnish with flowers, if using, before serving.

CHESTNUT SABLE

Makes enough for one tart

11.3 oz/320 g butter, soft
7.1 oz/202 g confectioners' sugar
4.2 oz/119 g eggs
14.1 oz/400 g all-purpose flour
2.6 oz/74 g chestnut flour
3.4 oz/95 g corn starch
¾ tsp/3 g kosher salt

1. In the bowl of a stand mixer fitted with a paddle attachment, combine the butter and sugar. Add half the eggs and mix to incorporate, scraping down the sides, as needed. Add the remaining eggs and mix to combine.
2. Add the flours, corn starch, and salt and mix just until homogenous. Wrap and refrigerate overnight.
3. On a floured surface, roll the dough to ¼-inch thick and cut to fit a 12-inch by 5-inch tart pan (or 8-in or 9-inch round). Extra dough can be reserved for another use.
4. Transfer to a silicone-lined baking sheet and refrigerate for 15 minutes.
5. Preheat the oven to 350°F.
6. Bake the tart shell until golden brown all over, about 15 minutes. Set aside to cool completely.

CHESTNUT CONFIT

Make enough for one tart

7.1 oz/200 g water
10.6 oz/300 g sugar
3.5 oz/100 g shelled chestnuts

1. Combine the water and sugar in a saucepan and bring to a boil over medium heat. Add the chestnuts and reduce to a simmer.
2. Simmer the chestnuts until tender and a paring knife slides through easily, about 10 minutes.
3. Cool completely before using.

TURBAN SQUASH DIPLOMAT CREAM

Makes enough for one tart

4.4 oz/125 g sugar
1.8 oz/50 g corn starch
4.2 oz/120 g egg yolks
8.8 oz/250 g milk
1 vanilla bean, split and seeds scraped
1.8 oz/50 g unsalted butter
1 tsp/1 g kosher salt
8.8 oz/250 g roasted turban squash
.1 oz/2 g silver gelatin sheets, bloomed in ice cold water
1 lb 1.6 oz/500 g heavy cream, whipped to soft peaks

1. Combine the sugar and starch in a large heat-safe bowl. Whisk to break up any lumps. Add the yolks and whisk until smooth.
2. Meanwhile, bring the milk and vanilla bean to a boil. While whisking the eggs constantly, stream about 1/4 of the milk mixture into the bowl with the eggs. Return to the pot with the remaining milk, whisking constantly, and bring to a hard boil until the mixture is smooth and thickened, about 4 minutes. Remove from the heat and add the gelatin sheets (without the soaking water).
3. Place the butter and salt in the bowl of a stand mixer fitted with the paddle attachment. Pour the hot custard over the butter and mix on medium speed until room temperature. Add the squash and mix until incorporated and somewhat smooth.
4. Remove from the mixer and fold the whipped cream in by hand.
5. Transfer to a piping bag.

ROASTING VEGETABLES

Thick-skinned whole vegetables, such as some root vegetables, winter squash, and eggplant, are well suited to roasting or baking. The skins protect the interior from drying or scorching. Roasting is also excellent for halved, cut, sliced, or diced vegetables. Rinse, peel, trim, and cut the vegetable, as necessary. To assure even cooking, cut vegetables into uniform pieces. Toss the vegetables with oil to promote browning and prevent excessive drying and scorching.

1. Prepare the vegetables for roasting as appropriate by type or intended use, and arrange them cut-side down in a preheating baking or roasting pan. Cut or sliced vegetables may be seasoned with salt, pepper, spices, oils, juices, or marinades.

   Add some liquid to the pan to steam dense vegetables and to prevent them from becoming overly brown or scorching as they roast. Set vegetables on racks over the liquid, or directly in the liquid, as preferred. Ideally, the liquid should all evaporate toward the end of the cooking process to achieve quality factors consistent with roasted items, so use just enough to cover the surface of the pan, and add more only if needed.

2. Place the vegetables in a medium to hot oven and roast to the desired doneness.

   The longer the roasting time (a factor determined by the type of vegetable, size and thickness, diameter of the cut, and its density), the lower the temperature of the oven should be. Vegetables may be roasted on sheet pans or in roasting pans or, in some cases, directly on the oven rack to allow the hot air to circulate readily. Generally, roasted vegetables are done when they can be pierced easily with the tip of a knife or kitchen fork.

   Vegetables should be rotated as they roast to promote even cooking, because most ovens have hot spots. Stir or turn the vegetables to keep those on the edge of the sheet pan from scorching. If the pan was covered, remove the cover or foil during the final stage of cooking to development a rich, roasted flavor and color.

PERSIMMON TARTE TATIN

Makes one 6-inch tart

There is a small variety of persimmons that grow in New York, called American Persimmons. The tree grows very tall, and you will need a ladder to harvest, but they are worth the effort. Ripe persimmons are very sweet, but if they aren't quite ready, they are surprisingly astringent—to the point that you'll need a drink of water from how overwhelmingly dry your mouth will feel!

12 oz/340 g Tallow Puff Pastry (page 199)

1 lb 1.6 oz/500 g sugar

5 to 6 American Persimmons, sliced and deseeded

10.6 oz/300 g apple cider

1.8 oz/50g Kampot peppercorns, crushed

1. Preheat the oven to 400°F/205°C.
2. On a floured surface, roll the dough to ¼-inch and cut a 6-inch circle.
3. Transfer the circle to a silicone-lined baking sheet. Use a fork or dough docker to dock the dough all over.
4. Bake until the circle is golden brown all over and crisp, about 15 minutes. Set aside to cool completely.
5. In a heavy bottomed saucepan over medium heat, cook the sugar without stirring until it dissolves and turns golden brown, about 5 minutes. Add the persimmons.
6. Deglaze the pan with about one third of the apple cider, and continue cooking until the persimmons are soft, deglazing the pan as needed with additional cider, 10 to 15 minutes.
7. Place the baked puff pastry on a serving plate or cake circle. Top with the persimmons and pour the remaining caramel over the persimmons.
8. Garnish with peppercorns.

BAKED ANTIQUE APPLES WITH CRÈME BRÛLÉE DIPLOMAT CREAM AND KOUSA DOGWOOD BERRIES

Makes 5 servings

5 silken apples (or other antique variety), halved and cored
3.5 oz/100 g cubed (there should be one cube per apple)
.7 oz/20 g Calvados or local apple brandy
7.1 oz/200 g apple cider
2.3 oz/65 g brown sugar

CRÈME BRÛLÉE DIPLOMAT CREAM (RECIPE BELOW)
8 oz/227 g soft-ripened bloomy rind cheese, like Camembert or brie, cubed
10 Kousa dogwood berries, skinned and pitted

Antique apple varieties are very flavorful and different than the generic apples we see all over the grocery stores from state-to-state. Seeking out and discovering new apple varieties is worth the effort, and you'll find flavors that you've never experienced in an apple. I paired the apples and crème brûlée cream with kousa dogwood berries, which had a flavor like persimmons and mangos and jammy texture when eaten. They grow everywhere and are for more than the birds.

1. Preheat the oven to 350°F/175°C.
2. Arrange the apples flesh-side up in a baking dish. Place a cube of butter in the center of each apple piece.
3. In a bowl, mix together the Calvados, cider, and brown sugar, and pour over the apples.
4. Cover the dish with foil and transfer to the oven for 15 minutes.
5. Remove from the oven and baste the apples with the liquid that has accumulated in the pan.
6. Return to the oven uncovered and cook until the apples are tender and easily pierced with a knife.
7. To serve, place two apple halves flesh-side up on a plate. Pipe enough diplomat cream to nearly cover the face of each apple. Top each with a cube of cheese and a small spoonful of berries.

CRÈME BRÛLÉE DIPLOMAT CREAM

Makes about 2 lb 1.5 oz/950 g

6.3 oz/180 g brown sugar
1 lb 5 oz/596 g milk
3.5 oz/99 g egg yolks
1.9 oz/54 g flan powder
2.6 oz/74 g butter
1 vanilla bean

15 oz/426 g whipped cream
.2 oz/7 g gelatin sheets

1. Spread the brown sugar on a silicone baking mat on a heat-safe surface. Using a kitchen torch, burn the sugar until it is very dark and smells like burned sugar. Set aside to cool.
2. In a heat-safe bowl, combine the yolks and flan powder. Set aside.
3. Bring the milk to a boil in a saucepan over moderate heat. Whisking constantly, pour about one third of the hot milk mixture into the bowl with the yolks and flan powder. Return the mixture to the pot while continuing to whisk.
4. Add the burned sugar and return to a boil, whisking constantly until the mixture has thickened, about 3 minutes.
5. Remove from the heat and strain into a bowl. Stir in the butter, and set aside to cool slightly.
6. Meanwhile, soak the gelatin in ice water until soft, about 8 minutes. Squeeze out any excess water.
7. Weigh the pastry cream and place 1 lb 4 oz/568 g in a large bowl with the strained gelatin and stir to melt. Fold in the whipped cream.
8. Transfer to a piping bag with a round tip (804).

RIPE PLUMS WITH FROMAGE BLANC, DILL, AND BEE POLLEN

Makes 10 servings

Just like apples, plums come in a wide variety of shapes, colors, and flavors. Some are sweeter than others, and for this recipe, I prefer a plum that is sweet and juicy, though any plum you love the most is the best to showcase. The tang of the fromage blanc helps to balance the sweetness in the fruit, and the olive oil brings everything together on your palate.

1. In a bowl, combine the sugar, lemon juice, lime juice, yogurt, sour cream, and fromage blanc.
2. Place a serving of the fromage blanc crème on a plate. Place a plum half on the crème, cut side up. Top with the honeycomb, dill fronds, and bee pollen before serving.

FROMAGE BLANC CRÈME
6.5 oz / 184 g sugar
1 oz / 25 g lemon juice
.6 oz / 16 g lime juice
4.1 oz / 117 g low-fat yogurt
7.1 oz / 201 g sour cream
8.9 oz / 251 g fromage blanc

5 ripe plums, halved and pitted
10 small pieces of honeycomb
10 sprigs dill
Bee pollen, as needed for garnish

WILDFLOWER LOLLIPOPS

Makes about 2 dozen lollipops, depending on size

14.1 oz/400 g granulated sugar
2.8 oz/80 g water
½ tsp/5 g lemon essence
¼ tsp/2 g citric acid
Edible wildflowers, such as snap dragons, daisies, borage, marigolds, and zinnias, as needed

I am an edible flower evangelist, and I do not think there is a better way to showcase our most beautiful ingredients than in crystal clear lollipops. And because flowers taste as good as they look, using a variety in your lollipops will be not just visually stunning, but a real treat.

1. Place small tart rings or round cookie cutters on a silicone baking mat-lined sheet tray. Coat the rings with vegetable oil. Place flowers inside the rings and set aside.
2. In a medium pot, bring the sugar and water to a boil. Use a wet pastry brush to wash the sides of the pot with water to remove any sugar on the sides to prevent crystallization. Once the mixture comes to a boil, do not stir or otherwise agitate the sugar.
3. Cook the sugar mixture to 300°F/149°C. Carefully pour the sugar into the ring molds to cover the flowers (reserve a few tablespoons worth of sugar in the pan). Let cool, and once the sugar is set, lift the rings up to remove.
4. To adhere sticks, warm the remaining sugar in the pot until it is soft. Dip the ends of the sticks in the sugar and then press against the back of the candy to adhere.
5. Serve right away or store in a well-sealed container or individually wrapped.

LILAC JELLY

Makes 4 pints

Lilacs are a beautiful spring flower adored by most but eaten by few. When I first used the lilacs to make jam, I was putting it on everything—English muffins, layers of cake, even peanut butter sandwiches! It is an easy and versatile recipe. If you use the dark purple flowers, you will get the purple you see in the photo. If you use lighter blossoms, or even white, the jam will still taste delicious, but it will be more of a brown color. The flavor of the jam is unique: it doesn't taste the way a lilac smells, instead it is fruity with a floral background.

7.1 oz/200g lilac blossoms, green parts removed
2 lb 1.4 oz/946g water
1.4 oz/40g lemon juice
1 lb 12.2 oz/800g sugar
2 oz/57 g powdered apple pectin

1. Place the lilac blossoms in a large heat-safe bowl.
2. Bring the water to a boil and pour over the lilacs. Set aside to infuse for 4 hours. It should be a turquoise color.
3. Strain the lilac tea into a saucepan. Add the lemon juice, which will not only change the color of the tea to pink, but is also required to balance the sugar in the recipe and help the pectin set, so don't skip the lemon.
4. Bring the mixture to a boil and add the pectin, stirring to dissolve. Allow the mixture to boil for 1 minute. (Note: Do not add the sugar at the same time as the pectin, or before the pectin, or the gel will not set.)
5. Add the sugar, stirring to dissolve. Bring the mixture back to a full boil for 1 minute .
6. Cool and store covered in the refrigerator.

PEACH AND WINEBERRY FRUIT LEATHER

Makes about 20 servings, depending on size

10 oz/283g g wineberries
14.5 oz/412 g white peaches, skin on
4.9 oz/138 g Gala apple, skin on
6.2 oz/175 g sugar

Wineberries look and taste like raspberries, with a deeper color and a touch more tartness. They are an invasive species in the Hudson Valley and across the northeast, growing on the roadside where you've likely not noticed them. I like pairing them with peaches since they grow at the same time of the season. These fruit leathers retain the vibrant fruit flavor for a handy, on-the-go snack for a hike or other adventure.

1. Preheat the oven to 150°F/65°C.
2. In a blender, purée the wineberries, peaches, apple, and sugar. Spread on a silicone-lined baking sheet.
3. Transfer to the oven and bake until fully set, about 24 hours.
4. Cool fully before cutting into strips and transferring to an air-tight container for storage.

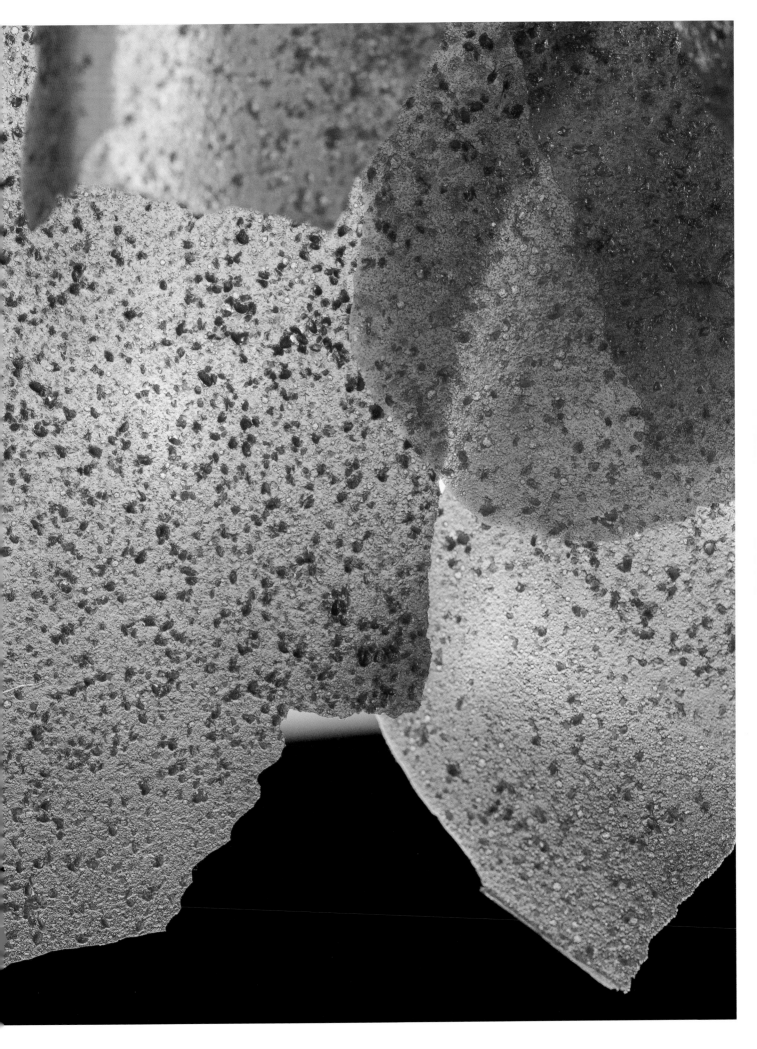

UMAMI CHOCOLATE BAR WITH MORELS

Makes about 5 bars, depending on size

We primarily think of mushrooms as a flavorful edition to a savory dish, but mushrooms are so much more versatile than that. This chocolate will not immediately taste of mushroom—the flavor will not hit you in the face. What I wanted in this bar was for the umami (the savory taste we love in mushrooms) to be front and center, making your mouth water for the very subtle taste of something savory. The more you eat it, the more mushroom-forward it becomes as the ganache plays tricks on your palate. I've used dried morels here because that's what I typically have available from my previously-foraged supply.

1. In a medium saucepan, bring the cream to a heavy simmer. Remove from the heat. Add the morels and cover. Set aside to steep for about 15 minutes. Use an immersion blender to blend the mushrooms in the cream. Strain; remeasure the cream and add any additional to return to the original weight, if needed, and return to the pot.

2. Meanwhile, in a heat-safe bowl, combine the milk chocolate, 100% chocolate, cocoa butter, white miso, and salt.

3. Bring the cream to a boil over moderate heat and pour over the chocolate mixture. Let sit for about 5 minutes, then blend with an immersion blender. Set aside to cool to about 32°C/90°F.

4. Pour into chocolate molds. Leave out at room temperature overnight to allow the ganache to crystallize.

5. The next day, top the bars in the mold with a thin layer of tempered chocolate. Allow it to set fully before unmolding.

1 lb 5.2 oz/600 g heavy cream, plus more as needed
.9 oz/25 g dried morel mushrooms
1 lb 1.6 oz/500 g milk chocolate
.6 oz/18 g 100% chocolate (cocoa mass)
1.2 oz/35 g cocoa butter
.5 oz/14 g sweet white miso
1 tsp/5 g kosher salt
Tempered milk chocolate, as needed for finishing

TAPIOCA PUDDING WITH PAW PAW GELÉE AND TOMATO JAM

Makes about 8 servings

TAPIOCA PUDDING

1.8 oz/50 g tapioca
10.6 oz/ 300 g milk
1½ tsp/5 g kosher salt
3.5 oz/100 g eggs
4.2 oz/120 g sugar

72% chocolate shavings, as needed for
  layering
Paw Paw Gelée (recipe follows)
Tomato Jam (recipe follows)

Pawpaw grows wild throughout the United States in abundance. With an appearance similar to a large mango and a flavor that combines banana, pineapple, and mango, it is an exciting fruit to discover. In the Hudson Valley, pawpaw is in season with the last of the tomatoes, and they pair beautifully.

1. For the pudding: place the tapioca in a covered container. Add enough water to cover the tapioca. Cover and refrigerate overnight. Strain before using.
2. The next day, in a medium saucepan, bring the milk, salt, and strained tapioca to a simmer. Cook until the tapioca is tender, about 20 minutes.
3. Meanwhile, in medium heat-safe bowl, whisk together the eggs and sugar. Once the tapioca is tender, whisk about 1 cup of the hot tapioca mixture into the eggs, whisking constantly. Pour the blended egg mixture into the pot, whisking constantly, and stir until combined. Remove from the heat and set aside to cool.
4. To assemble the desserts: in 8 glass serving vessels, place a layer of chocolate shavings. Evenly distribute the rice pudding over the shavings.
5. In a bowl, mix the gelée cubes with tomato jam, then place that mixture over the rice pudding. Finish each with another layer of chocolate shavings before serving.

PAW PAW GELÉE

Makes enough for one recipe

.7 oz/20 g gelatin
2 lb 3.3 oz/1000 g paw paw, peeled,
  deseeded, and cubed
3.5 oz/100 g water
7.1 oz/200 g sugar

1. In a small bowl, add the gelatin and enough very cold water to cover. Stir to combine, then set aside until the gelatin is rehydrated, at least 8 minutes.
2. In a blender, combine the paw paw and water. Blend until smooth.
3. Transfer the paw paw purée to a saucepan and add the sugar. Bring to a boil over moderate heat. Remove from the heat and add the rehydrated gelatin.
4. Place the pot into an ice water bath to cool and thicken the mixture slightly. Pour into a silicone-lined 13-in by 18-inch baking sheet. Once fully cooled and set, slice the gelée into small cubes.

TOMATO JAM

Makes enough for one recipe

10.6 oz/300 g tomato, roughly chopped
4.4 oz/125 g sugar, divided use
.5 oz/15 g apple pectin
1.8 oz/50 g lemon juice

1. In a pot, combine the tomato and 3.5oz/100 g of the sugar. Bring to a boil, stirring occasionally.
2. In a small bowl, stir together the pectin with the remaining .9oz/25 g sugar. Add to the tomato mixture, stirring until well combined. Remove from the heat and add the lemon juice. Set aside to cool fully.

CORN ICE CREAM WITH BLACKBERRIES

Makes 10 servings

Corn is sweet enough to be dessert on its own, but grilling or roasting gives it a smoky, savory depth of flavor that puts it over the top in this sweet and savory dessert. I've added some kiwi berries, which are in the same growing season as corn and blackberries, as well as a fennel frond and some edible flowers for a little extra garnish, but you can serve yours however you like.

1. Place the corn on a grill set to moderate heat. Grill the corn, turning frequently, until cooked and browned all over, about 10 minutes. Remove and set aside to cool to the touch, then cut the kernels from the cobs, reserving the kernels and cobs separately.
2. Transfer the kernels to a covered container with the milk. Use an immersion blender to blend the kernels until mostly smooth. Add the corn cobs and cover. Refrigerate for 24 hours to infuse.
3. Strain the milk mixture (reserve the cobs to use in Biscuit with Corn Cob Syrup, page 6), and reweigh the milk. Add more as needed to return to the original weight.
4. In a large heavy-bottomed pot, bring the corn-milk and cream to a boil over moderate heat. Add the sugar, milk powder, glucose powder, and stabilizer. Stir and return to a boil.
5. Place the egg yolks in a heat-safe bowl. While whisking constantly, pour about 1 cup of the hot milk mixture into the eggs. Once incorporated, pour this mixture back into the pot, whisking constantly.
6. Return to a simmer. Remove from the heat and strain. Cool completely.
7. Spin the cooled corn base into an ice cream machine according to the manufacturer's instructions, working in batches, if needed. Transfer the ice cream to covered containers and freeze until needed.
8. To assemble, dollop the blackberry chantilly in the bottom of a serving bowl. Top with a scoop of ice cream and some celery curls. Finish with kiwi berries, fennel fronds, and edible flowers, if you like.

ROASTED CORN ICE CREAM
2 ears of corn
1 lb 4.2 oz/574 g whole milk, plus more as needed
5.4 oz/154 g heavy cream
4.6 oz/130 g sugar
1.2 oz/33 g milk powder
1.3 oz/38 g glucose powder
.2 oz/11 g stabilizer
1.2 oz/34 g egg yolks

Blackberry Chantilly (recipe below)
Celery Curls (recipe below)

BLACKBERRY CHANTILLY

Makes 10 servings

1. Combine the cream, blackberry purée, and sugar. Whip by hand or with a mixer until medium peaks form. Refrigerate until needed.

10.6 oz/300 g heavy cream
3.5 oz/100 g blackberries, puréed
1.4 oz/40 g sugar

CELERY CURLS

Makes 10 servings

1. Bring the water, sugar, and vanilla bean (seeds and pod) to a boil in a medium saucepan.
2. Add the celery and cook until vibrant green, about 20 seconds.
3. Remove from the heat and set aside to cool in the syrup.

1 lb 4.5 oz/580 g water
2.5 oz/70 g brown sugar
1 vanilla bean, scraped
1.2 oz/34 g celery curls, shaved with a vegetable peeler

MAPLE PHYLLO CUSTARD WITH BOURBON BROWN BUTTER PECAN ICE CREAM AND POACHED CRANBERRIES

Makes 15 servings

4.4 oz/125 g milk

1.1 oz/30 g maple syrup, plus more as needed for finishing

6.2 oz/175 g sweetened condensed milk

½ tsp/2 g kosher salt

1.8 oz/50 g eggs

One (1 lb) box phyllo dough

Melted butter, as needed (use the reserved brown butter from the Butter Pecans)

Bourbon Brown Butter Pecan Ice Cream (recipe below)

Poached Cranberries (recipe below)

In New York state, maple syrup, cranberries, and pecans are a classic combination of ingredients all grown right here. Inspired by a maple-based pecan pie, this recipe bakes a silky maple custard right into the "crust" of buttered and crisp phyllo dough. It's a twist on classic flavors with a unique presentation.

1. Preheat the oven to 350°F/177°C.
2. In a blender, blend the milk, syrup, condensed milk, salt, and eggs until smooth. Set aside.
3. Place on sheet of phyllo on a clean work surface. Brush it with the butter and top with a second piece of phyllo dough. Brush the second sheet of phyllo with butter.
4. Gather the phyllo and allow it to crinkle in your hands until you have a long bunch of the dough. Place it in a 10-in by 12-inch baking pan.
5. Repeat the process until the pan is full, ensuring the bunches are tucked close together.
6. Brush the top of the phyllo with maple syrup.
7. Transfer to the oven and bake for 10 minutes. Remove from the oven and brush with more maple syrup. Bake for 10 more minutes.
8. Remove from the oven and pour the reserved egg mixture over the phyllo dough. Reduce the temperature to 300°F/150°C.
9. Return to the oven and bake until the custard is set, about 10 minutes.
10. Cool for about 10 minutes before serving hot or warm with butter pecan ice poached cranberries.

POACHED CRANBERRIES

2.8 oz/80 g cranberries

5.3 oz/150 g sugar

2.8 oz/80 g water

Makes about 3 oz/85 g cranberries

1. Prick the cranberries so each is pricked 3 to 5 times.
2. In a medium saucepan, bring the water and sugar to a simmer. Add the cranberries and simmer gently until tender and almost translucent, 3 to 4 minutes.
3. Remove from the heat and set aside to cool in the syrup.

PECAN BOURBON ICE CREAM

Makes 15 servings

3.2 oz/90 g egg yolks
4.6 oz/130 g sugar
1 lb 2 oz/516 g milk
5.8 oz/165 g heavy cream
.7 oz/19 g trimoline or honey
1.8 oz/50 g milk powder
.1oz/2 g ice cream stabilizer (optional)
1 oz/29 g bourbon
Butter Pecans (recipe below)

1. Combine the eggs and ⅓ of the sugar in a heat-safe bowl; set aside.
2. In a heavy-bottomed saucepan over moderate heat, combine the milk, cream, and trimoline and bring to a boil.
3. Meanwhile, combine the milk powder, stabilizer (if using), and the remaining sugar. Stir together.
4. Stream the milk powder mixture into the milk, stirring constantly. Return to a boil.
5. Pour about ⅓ of the milk mixture into the bowl with the eggs, whisking constantly until incorporated. Puur this mixture back into the pot, whisking constantly.
6. Switch to a wooden spoon or spatula, and stir until the sauce thickens slightly and coats the back of the spoon, about 5 minutes. Remove from the heat and add the bourbon.
7. Cool, then transfer to a covered container and refrigerate overnight.
8. Spin the ice cream base in an ice cream machine according to the manufacturer's directions. Empty the ice cream into a large bowl and fold in the butter pecans.
9. Transfer to storage containers and freeze until needed.

BUTTER PECANS

Makes enough for one batch of ice cream

5.3 oz/150 g pecans
3.5 oz/100 g brown butter
½ tsp/2.5 g kosher salt

1. Preheat the oven to 350°F/177°C. Spread the pecans on a baking sheet and transfer to the oven. Roast until the pecans are golden brown and fragrant, about 10 minutes.
2. Transfer the hot pecans to a large bowl with the brown butter and salt. Sift over a small bowl, reserving excess brown butter for use later.
3. Return the pecans to the baking sheet and lower the oven to 325°F/160°C.
4. Bake until toasted all over, about 10 more minutes. Remove and cool, then transfer to the freezer until needed.

WORKING WITH PHYLLO DOUGH

Prepared phyllo dough is available in the freezer section of supermarkets and from Greek or Middle Eastern groceries.

Thaw frozen phyllo dough either in the refrigerator overnight or at room temperature for 2 hours. Once thawed, the individual sheets should pull apart easily and be very flexible. However, contact with the air soon dries out phyllo unless it is covered.

Set up your work area so that your phyllo stays moist and flexible as you work with it. Place a large baking sheet or a piece of plastic wrap on your work surface, remove the phyllo from the box, and unroll enough sheets to make your recipe. Set the sheets flat on the baking sheet or plastic wrap. Cover the sheets completely with another large piece of plastic wrap, then lay lightly dampened paper towels or a barely moistened kitchen towel over the plastic to keep the air around the phyllo moist.

Transfer one sheet of the phyllo at a time to your flat work area and immediately re-cover the remaining sheets. Brush or spray the entire sheet with butter or oil. Your sheets may tear or crease as you transfer them or brush them with fat. That's okay; the many layers of phyllo hide imperfections.

Keep working this way, one sheet at a time, until you have the correct number of layers for your recipe. Let the shaped or filled phyllo chill in the refrigerator before baking for the lightest, flakiest layers.

CONCORD GRAPE SPAGHETTI SQUASH PLATED DESSERT

Makes 7 servings

Grape Sorbet (recipe follows)
Roasted Spaghetti Squash (recipe follows)
Pistachio Crumble (recipe follows)
Freshly cracked black pepper, for garnish
7 Cured Egg Yolks (page 195)

I am a huge fan of concord grapes, which have a short growing season. When we have them, I like to juice them to store in my freezer for the year. You can use the juice to make jam, jelly, pie, ice cream, and more. When you're straining juice from the grapes, you may need to process them twice to press all the juice from the skins. Concord grapes grow seasonally alongside spaghetti squash, which is underutilized in desserts, so I've incorporated them both here with some of my other favorite flavors and plenty of texture.

1. To assemble the desserts, place a scoop of sorbet on each plate. Surround with spaghetti squash, as desired, then pistachio crumble.
2. Finish with pepper and an egg yolk before serving.

GRAPE SORBET

Makes 7 servings

GRAPE SORBET BASE
1 lb 5.2 oz/600 g water
4.4 oz/125 g sugar (first)
.4 oz/10 g sorbet stabilizer
15.4 oz/438 g sugar (second)
4.4 oz/125 g glucose powder

SORBET
1 lb 15.7 oz/900 sorbet base
2 lb 14 oz/1300 g concord grape juice

1. For the sorbet base, bring the water to a boil in a medium pot over moderate heat. Stir in the first sugar and sorbet stabilizer, then return to a boil. Add the second sugar and glucose powder and return to a boil. Strain, and set aside to cool.
2. For the sorbet, combine the base and grape juice and spin in an ice cream machine according to manufacturer's directions. Transfer to a container and freeze until needed.

SPAGHETTI SQUASH

Makes enough for one batch of desserts

1 small spaghetti squash, halved and
  deseeded
2 oz/60 g vegetable oil
12 oz sweetened condensed milk,
  divided use

1. Preheat the oven to 400°F/204°C.
2. Place the spaghetti squash pulp-side up on a baking sheet. Rub the squash with oil, then brush with half of the condensed milk.
3. Roast until beginning to brown and caramelize, about 30 minutes. Remove from the oven and brush with the remaining condensed milk.
4. Return to the oven and bake until tender, about 20 minutes more. Remove from the oven and set aside to cool.
5. Once cool, scrape the pulp with a fork to make strands that look like pasta. Set aside.

PISTACHIO CRUMBLE

Makes enough for one batch of desserts

4 oz New York-grown (or, local to you)
  shelled pistachios
2.3 oz/65 g sugar
1.3 oz/38 g all-purpose flour
3.4 tsp/4 g kosher salt
.7 oz/20 g melted butter

1. Preheat the oven to 300°F/150°C.
2. In the bowl of a food processor, pulse the nuts until crumbly. Add the sugar, flour, salt, and butter, and blend until a crumble forms.
3. Bake until golden brown and crisp, 10 to 15 minutes.

MAKING MAGIC WITH HONEYBEES

For chefs with an interest in sustainability, there is no better practice than beekeeping. Pollinators are at the base of the food system we all rely on. An estimated 40% of all plant foods rely on pollinators, whose populations are in decline globally. Honeybees are the easiest to see because they conveniently bunch up so we can spot when they vanish, but other pollinators, including butterflies, are in trouble, too.

On campus at The Culinary Institute of America (CIA) in Hyde Park, New York, we have The Apiary, a small enclosure in a former pavilion that's been turned into a drought tolerant, pollinator-friendly garden. We currently have three beehives housing upwards of 50,000 bees each. Keeping them alive is a struggle—bees have so many challenges these days. They suffer from loss of habitat, pesticides, weedkillers, increasing numbers of aggressive parasites, and industrial beekeeping practices that leave them malnourished and disoriented. If our pollinator populations weren't in trouble, though, we wouldn't feel that it was as urgently necessary to teach our students about them.

Our pollinator hotel allows students to get familiar with our solitary pollinator species, along with the beehives. Our gardens grow herbs that are tasty for humans and provide excellent food sources for butterflies. You will find students down there often, watching the hives and reading, studying, or just taking a break in the garden. The Apiary helps to make the campus gardens more productive and provides honey for student projects and tastings.

CARAMELIZED SECKEL PEARS WITH BEER CREAM AND SUNFLOWER SEEDS

Makes 4 servings

Seckel pears are smaller than other pears, but they are just as crisp and juicy. There is no need to peel the pears; I enjoy the texture of the skin once it is roasted, and it helps the pears keep their shape. The addition of sunflower seeds adds a toasty nut-free flavor that marries with the hoppy malt in the beer and the

1. Spread the mascarpone beer cream on a dessert plate. Place two pear halves over the cream.
2. Sprinkle the pears with the seeds, salt, and petals before serving.

Caramelized Pears (recipe below)
Mascarpone Beer Cream(recipe below)
Toasted sunflower seeds, as needed for garnish
Maldon sea salt flakes, as needed for garnish
Sunflower petals (optional), as needed for garnish

CARAMELIZED PEARS

1. Place the sugar in a heavy skillet over low heat and stir until the sugar dissolves. Slowly cook to a light golden brown without stirring, about 4 minutes.
2. Add the pears, skin-side up, and continue to cook until the caramel is a medium golden color, about 2 more minutes, and add a splash of the pear cider.
3. Continue cooking until the skin begins to darken, and then add the remaining cider to deglaze the pan. Continue cooking until the pears are tender, about 5 minutes.
4. Remove from the heat and set aside to cool.

3.5 oz/100 g sugar
4 seckel pears, cored and halved
10.6 oz/300 g pear cider

MASCARPONE BEER CREAM

1. In a bowl, combine the cream and beer and whip until soft, but still soupy. Refrigerate until needed.
2. Place the eggs in a mixer fitted with the whip attachment and whip until they are pale yellow and slightly thickened.
3. In a saucepan, add the sugar and enough water to make the consistency of wet sand. Bring a boil, and without stirring, cook until the sugar is 240°F/115°C. Remove from the heat.
4. With the mixer on medium-low speed, slowly stream in the hot sugar. Beat until the mixture has doubled in size and is just barely warm.
5. Add the softened mascarpone and whip until the mixture is completely smooth, with no visible lumps.
6. Remove from the mixer and fold in the cream mixture until just combined. Refrigerate until ready to use.

13 oz/367 g heavy cream
2.1 oz/60 g stout beer
3.6 oz/103 g egg yolks
5.4 oz/154 g sugar
13 oz/367 g mascarpone, slightly warmed in the microwave or stovetop

NOT-RED VELVET CAKE

Makes 3 to 4 servings

Camembert Brûlée (recipe below)
Roasted Beets (recipe below)
5 champagne grapes, sliced
Roasted walnuts, roughly chopped
2 Black Bean Sesame Cakes (page 55),
   or other chocolate cake, broken into
   bite-size pieces
Dark (66%) dark chocolate shavings, as
   needed for garnish

This is a shareable dessert inspired by a cake I don't particularly care for. Red velvet cake is just not for me, but I enjoy all the components in other ways—and that's where this cheese course meets dessert comes in. There is chocolate cake, beets (they are, in fact, red), and Camembert instead of cream cheese frosting. It is the perfect last bite for not-dessert-people.

1. Place the camembert on a serving plate. Surround with beets, grapes, walnuts, and pieces of cake. Finish with chocolate shavings before serving.

1 (8 oz) Camembert cheese
1 oz/25 g sugar

CAMEMBERT BRÛLÉE

1. Use a sharp knife to cut the top from the cheese. Sprinkle sugar over the exposed cheese. Use a kitchen torch to melt and brown the sugar.

4 small beets
1 oz/25 g olive oil
1 ½ tsp/8 g kosher salt
.5 oz/12 g freshly cracked black pepper

ROASTED BEETS

1. Preheat the oven to 400°F/205°C.
2. Place the beets in a baking dish or casserole. Rub all over with the oil and season with salt and pepper.
3. Roast until the beets are tender and a skewer through the center comes out easily, about 1 hour.
4. Remove from the oven and cool slightly, then use a clean towel to rub the beets and remove the skin. Cut into eighths and reserve.

Chapter 4: Grains

GRAINS ARE A POWERHOUSE OF complex carbohydrates, the primary fuel source for our bodies. They provide a steady release of energy, helping to sustain vitality throughout the day. Grains are packed with fiber, which plays a vital role in digestive health, promoting a healthy gut microbiome. Fiber also helps to lower cholesterol levels, reducing the risk of heart disease and stroke, making grains a valuable component of a balanced diet.

If you aren't already sold, grains are also brimming with essential vitamins and minerals, like B vitamins, iron, magnesium, and zinc, which are vital for various bodily functions. Whole grains, in particular, are rich in antioxidants, which help to combat inflammation in the body. These antioxidants have been linked to a reduced risk of chronic diseases, including certain cancers and cardiovascular conditions.

It's worth noting that the type of grain matters. Whole grains, such as brown rice, quinoa, oats, and whole wheat, retain all parts of the grain kernel, including the bran, germ, and endosperm, thus preserving their nutrient content. Refined grains, on the other hand, undergo processing that strips away the bran and germ, resulting in a loss of fiber, vitamins, and minerals. Milling your own grains puts it in your hands, with flours from whole grains with all of the beneficial parts.

Ancient grains, such as quinoa, amaranth, and spelt, have been cultivated for centuries and offer unique nutritional profiles. Rich in protein, fiber, and essential nutrients, these grains are prized for their health benefits. Quinoa, for example, is considered a superfood, packing more minerals, protein, vitamins, and fiber than more popular grains like whole wheat.

Using these grains, either whole or as milled flours, in baking and pastry recipes introduces new flavor profiles and textures. Using alternative flours in place of standard all-purpose can have a drastic impact on the finished recipe, and experimenting with the vast catalogue of grains opens up a new door for variations on popular desserts (like the Kamut Khorasan Marshmallow Treats page 151), and ones we have yet to experience.

HUCKLEBERRY CORNBREAD

Makes one 18 – by 13-inch tray

1 oz/29 g milk
2.6 oz/75 g water
3.5 oz/100 g eggs
4.5 oz/128 g olive oil
9 oz/256 g sugar
3.7 oz/106 g amaranth flour
5.3 oz/150 g sorghum flour
3.8 oz/108 g cornmeal
.7 oz/21 g baking powder
1½ tsp/9 g kosher salt
7.9 oz/225 g huckleberries

You can find amaranth flour at some specialty markets, but if not, you can grind amaranth seeds in a powerful food processor, blender, or even better, a tabletop grain mill or attachment. Added to the amaranth and cornmeal, you'll have a gluten-free and nutrient-dense cornbread. I've added huckleberries here, but you can swap in any of your favorite fruits or savory mix-ins.

1. Preheat the oven to 350°F/175°C.
2. In a large bowl, combine the milk, water, eggs, and oil. Add the sugar, flours, cornmeal, baking powder, and salt, and mix until combined and homogenous.
3. Fold in the huckleberries.
4. Transfer to a greased 18 – by 13-inch pan. Bake until the bread is golden brown and bounces back when pressed lightly, about 25 minutes. Set aside to cool before slicing.

KAMUT KHORASAN SMOKED CINNAMON MARSHMALLOW TREATS

Makes 12 servings

Kamut is an ancient grain, guaranteed under the KAMUT® brand to never be modified or hybridized, always organically grown. Kamut has higher protein content than wheat, with more nutrients, like potassium, magnesium, and vitamin E. It can be puffed, just like rice, so I've used it here in a classic crispy marshmallow treat. This is a great way to normalize eating grains for kids, as well, so they can become accustomed to a variety of ingredients, through dessert!

1. In a medium saucepan, combine the Kamut with enough water to cover. Bring to a boil and cook until tender, about 15 minutes.
2. Drain the Kamut and spread on a baking sheet to cool and dry slightly. Pat dry with a clean towel.
3. Heat enough oil to fill a medium-size lidded pot about halfway. Add the cooked Kamut and cover. Cook, shaking the pan occasionally, while the Kamut pops. When the popping has slowed to a near stop, remove from the heat and pour on a towel to absorb any excess oil. Set aside.
4. In a small heat-safe bowl, combine the gelatin and ice water. Set aside.
5. In the bowl of a stand mixer fitted with a whip attachment, whip the egg whites on medium-low speed.
6. Meanwhile, in a small pot, combine the sorghum, water, and sugar. Cook over medium heat without stirring until the syrup reaches 245°F/115°C.
7. Remove from the heat and slowly stream the hot sugar mixture into the whipping egg whites.
8. While the egg whites whip, fill the pot used for the sugar syrup about 1/3 with water. Bring to a light simmer. Place the bowl with the gelatin over the pot to make a hot water bath. Add the honey and stir to dissolve. Remove from the heat and add the vanilla powder and cinnamon.
9. Stream the gelatin mixture into the whipping egg whites. Let the mixture whip until cooled. Remove from the mixer and stir in the popped Kamut.
10. Spread the mixture into a greased 9-in by 13-inch pan. Cut into 12 large squares. Dip in melted chocolate before serving.

8.8 oz/250 g Kamut Khorasan
Water, as needed
Vegetable oil, as needed for frying

2.6 oz/75 g sorghum syrup
3 oz/84 g water
10.6 oz/300 g sugar
4.6 oz/131 g egg whites

3 tsp/12½ g powdered gelatin
2 tbsp/30 g ice cold water
2.6 oz/75 g honey
1½ tsp/6 g vanilla extract
½ tsp/5 g smoked cinnamon

Melted dark chocolate, as needed

ANCIENT GRAIN SCOTCHAROOS

Makes 9 servings

5.3 oz/150 g puffed millet
12 oz/340 g sorghum syrup
7.1 oz/200 g sugar
8.8 oz/250 g peanut butter

GANACHE
7.9 oz/225 g dark chocolate, finely
  chopped
6.2 oz/175 g heavy cream
.9 oz/25 g sorghum syrup
1½ tsp/8 g kosher salt

I am always looking for ways to incorporate ancient grains into my day because of their health benefits. Millet is an ancient grain *superfood* which makes it perfect for any dessert to increase the nutrient density of the foods we love. I like the flavor of sorghum syrup over corn syrup, so I've used it here.

1. Spread the puffed millet over the bottom of a greased 9-in by 13-in baking dish. Set aside.

2. In a medium saucepan over low to medium-low heat, stir the sorghum syrup and sugar until the sugar is dissolved and no longer grainy. Do not bring to a boil.

3. Remove from the heat and stir in the peanut butter. Working quickly, pour the mixture over the puffed millet. Set aside to cool until set, about 20 minutes.

4. Meanwhile, prepare the ganache. Place the chocolate in a medium heat-safe bowl; set aside. In a saucepan, bring the cream, sorghum, and salt to a boil. Pour over the chocolate and blend with an immersion blender until smooth.

5. Pour the ganache over the set millet mixture. Let set at room temperature or in the refrigerator before slicing into squares.

TOMATO CHOCOLATE RUGELACH

Makes about 3 dozen

Tomato and chocolate may seem like an odd pair, but fruit and chocolate is a classic combination—and what is a tomato if not a fruit? With the addition of just enough sugar to help round out the sweetness of the tomatoes, the filling is rich and flavorful between layers of tender cream cheese dough.

1. For the rugelach, place the butter and cream cheese in the bowl of a stand mixer fitted with a paddle attachment. Mix on medium speed, scraping as needed, until smooth.
2. Add the flour and salt, and mix on low speed until the ingredients are mostly combined, but some butter is still visible.
3. Transfer the dough to a floured work surface and roll to ¼-inch thick. Fold the dough like a letter. Transfer to a baking sheet and refrigerate for at least 20 minutes.
4. Meanwhile, in a medium bowl, combine the chocolate and salt. Set aside.
5. Combine the tomatoes and sugar in a saucepan over high heat. Cook, stirring frequently, until the tomatoes break down and thicken.
6. When the tomato mixture is thick enough to spread, remove from the heat and pour over the chocolate. Let set for 1 minute, then stir to combine. Set aside to cool fully.
7. Preheat the oven to 350°F.
8. Transfer the chilled dough to a floured surface and roll the dough until it is ⅛-inch thick.
9. Divide the dough into 3 pieces. Working one piece at a time, on a floured surface, roll the dough into a circle that is ¼-inch thick. Use a pastry cutter or sharp knife to cut the dough into 4 quarters, then cut each quarter into thirds to make a total of 12 triangles that meet in the center.
10. Spread the dough with the filling, leaving about ½-inch border around the edges of the circle.
11. Roll each triangle from the outside toward the center, finishing with the tail at the bottom of the dough. Transfer to a silicone-lined baking sheet and continue with the remaining dough.
12. Bake until the rugelach are golden brown, about 20 minutes. Transfer to a rack to cool.

RUGELACH DOUGH

13½ oz/382 g cream cheese, softened
1 lb/454 g unsalted butter, room temperature
1 lb/454 g spelt flour
Pinch of kosher salt

TOMATO CHOCOLATE FILLING

5.3 oz/150 g dark (72%) chocolate, finely chopped
½ oz/10 g kosher salt
10.6 oz/300 g heirloom tomatoes, chopped
1.8 oz/50 g sugar

SORGHUM GRANOLA BARS

Makes 25 bars

1.9 oz/53 g shelled pistachios
2.1 oz/60 g pecans
3 oz/86 g rolled oats
2.1 oz/60 g sunflower seeds
2.1 oz/61 g dried cherries
3.1 oz/89 g dried apricots, chopped
1.4 oz/40 g golden raisins
1.1 oz/30 g flax seeds
1.4 oz/40 g sesame seeds
1 tsp/5 g sea salt

1.6 oz/45 g sugar
.6 oz/16 g water
3.6 oz/101 g sorghum syrup

.8 oz/22 g cocoa butter

Commercial granola bars are typically high in empty calories, which is the opposite of what makes granola bars so great! I like it when they are packed with nutrients from seeds, nuts, dried fruits to keep me energized when I'm in the kitchen or out hiking. I chose sorghum to replace corn syrup here for a little sweetness, since it is a source of antioxidants, fiber, vitamins, and minerals. Sweets can be sweet, but I like being intentional with how I sweeten.

1. Preheat the oven to 325°F. Spread the pistachios, pecans, and oats on a baking sheet. Roast, stirring occasionally, until golden brown, about 15 minutes. Transfer to a large bowl, and add the sunflower seeds, cherries, apricots, raisins, flax, sesame, and salt.
2. Meanwhile, in a saucepan, combine the water, sugar, and sorghum syrup. Cook until the mixture reaches 240°F on a candy thermometer.
3. Pour the syrup over the nut and fruit mixture and stir in the cocoa butter.
4. Lightly oil a silicone mat-lined baking sheet. Spread the granola mix into an even layer and cover. Leave to set overnight before slicing. Store wrapped or covered for up to 1 week.

SEMOLINA RICOTTA TART

Makes two 9-inch tarts

Semolina is made from durum wheat, and I've included both because I wanted two different textures while still making a dough that is 100% durum wheat. If you aren't ready to make two tarts, you can freeze one crust for later, either baked (and cooled) or raw, to be baked from frozen later.

1. In the bowl of a food processor, combine the flours and salt. Pulse to blend. Add the cold butter and pulse, scraping down the sides if needed, until it forms a mealy mixture with pea-sized pieces, about 15 seconds.
2. Continue pulsing as you stream in the water. Pulse until a dough forms, about 30 seconds. Take care not to overmix.
3. Form the dough into a ball and cover. Refrigerate for at least 1 hour.
4. Preheat the oven to 350°F/175°C.
5. Divide the dough into 2 pieces. On a floured surface, roll each piece of dough into a 10-inch circle. Crush off excess flour and transfer to a silicone-lined baking pan (you may need two baking pans). Pleat or fold the edges over to make a crust. Line within the crust with baking weights or dry beans and bake until lightly golden brown, 15 to 20 minutes. Cool fully.
6. In a small bowl, combine the ricotta and sugar. Spread on the bottom of the cooled tart. Top with berries and drizzle with olive oil, to taste.

8.7 oz/246 g durum flour
2.1 oz/60 g semolina
¾ tsp/4 g kosher salt
1 tbsp/18 g sugar
4.2 oz/120 g unsalted butter, cubed, cold
8 oz/227 g ice cold water

7.1 oz/200 g sheep's milk ricotta
.7 oz/20 g sugar
1 lb/454 g berries, like wild wine berries
Extra-virgin olive oil, as needed

CHERRY PIE WITH SPELT CRUST AND LEMON-THYME CHANTILLY

Makes one 10-inch pie

SPELT PIE CRUST
6 oz/170 g spelt flour
Pinch kosher salt
4 oz/113 g unsalted butter, cubed
½-inch and chilled
2 oz/57 g ice water

CHERRY PIE FILLING
8.8 oz/250 g cherry or apple juice
6 oz/170 g sugar
¾ tsp/4 g kosher salt
.9 oz/25 g potato starch
1 lb 4 oz/567 g sour cherries, hulled and
  quartered

LEMON THYME CHANTILLY
10.6 oz/300 g heavy cream
.5 oz/10 g lemon thyme

Lemon thyme leaves, for garnish
Lemon thyme flowers, for garnish

Use 1 oz of pie dough for every inch of pie pan.

You can make the same pie over and over and never tire of it. But for me, once I've gotten the hang of something, I love to see what else I can do to make it different and new. That's when I started experimenting with different flours in my pie crusts—and I especially like this 100% spelt version. Spelt adds nuttiness to the dough without actually adding any nuts.

1. For the pie crust, sift the flour and salt into a large bowl.
2. Cut the butter into the flour until pea sized pieces form. Add the cold water all at once. Mix until just combined.
3. Form the dough into a disk and wrap tightly. Refrigerate for at least an hour.
4. Preheat the oven to 425°F/218°C.
5. On a floured surface, roll the dough into a circle slightly larger than the pie pan. Brush off any excess flour and transfer to the pie pan. Roll the dough on a floured bench, brush off flour, line tin.
6. On a floured surface, roll the dough into a circle slightly larger than the pie pan. Brush off any excess flour and transfer to the pie pan. Crimp the edges of the dough. Dock the bottom of the dough with a fork and place on a baking sheet.
7. Bake the pie crust until golden brown and matte, about 20 minutes. Set aside to cool.
8. For the filling, combine about 80% of the juice with the sugar. Bring to a boil over moderate heat, stirring as needed.
9. 8. Meanwhile, in a small bowl, combine the remaining cherry juice with the starch to create a slurry. Stream the slurry into the boiling mixture. Return to a boil for 1 minute. Add the cherries and salt, and boil for another minute. Remove from the heat and set aside to cool completely.
10. Meanwhile, for the Chantilly, bring the cream to a simmer. Add the lemon thyme and steep for 5 minutes, adding additional time as needed for a strong flavor. If the mixture is bitter, it may have steeped too long, so keep tasting as it steeps. minutes. Strain and cool.
11. Whip the cooled cream until it holds its shape.
12. Spread the cooled cherry filling into the cooled pie crust. Use a round tip (806) to pipe along the edge of the pie. Garnish with the leaves and flowers.

AMARANTH QUICHE

Makes one 8-inch deep dish pie

Amaranth is often referred to as a grain, but it's actually a seed from the same family as beets, Swiss chard, and spinach. Using amaranth alongside sorghum flour creates a tender but sturdy dough that is particularly good for a hearty quiche.

1. In the bowl of a food processor, combine the flours and salt. Pulse to blend. Add the cold butter and pulse, scraping down the sides if needed, until the mixture is a coarse, sandy meal, about 15 seconds.
2. Continue pulsing as you stream in the water. Pulse until a dough forms, about 30 seconds. Take care not to overmix.
3. Transfer to a baking sheet. Cover and refrigerate for at least one hour.
4. Roll the dough to fit an 8-inch deep-dish ring mold. Grease the mold and line with the dough. Trim and transfer to the refrigerator to chill until firm to the touch.
5. Preheat the oven to 300°F/150°C.
6. Meanwhile, prepare the filling by blending the cream, eggs, yolk, and salt in a medium bowl. Whisk until well-combined.
7. Line the chilled crust with any inclusions, if using, and pour in the filling to the top of the mold.
8. Bake until the quiche is set and jiggles like gelatin, about one hour. Cool before slicing and serving.

PÂTE BRISÉE

13.7 oz/375 g white sorghum flour
13.7 oz/375 amaranth flour
.6 oz/18 g kosher salt
13.7 oz/375 g unsalted butter, cubed, cold
6.3 oz/180 g water

QUICHE BATTER

1 lb 2.7 oz/529 g cream
15.9 oz/450 g eggs
.9 oz/25 g egg yolk
1 tsp/5 g kosher salt
2 cups/473 mL inclusions, like leftover roasted vegetables or raw vegetable trim

OAT FUNNEL CAKES

Makes 12 servings

.9 oz/26 g sugar
7.1 oz/200 g oat flour
2 tsp/6 g kosher salt
2 tsp/8 g baking powder
1.8 oz/50 g eggs
8 oz/227 g milk
Vegetable oil, as needed for frying

Confectioners' sugar, for finishing

Oat flour is not inherently gluten-free since oats are processed alongside the rest of the wheat plant. However, special processing can produce gluten-free oats, and many oat flours are gluten-free, making these oat flour funnel cakes a crispy, gluten-free snack that anyone can enjoy. Oat flour is very mild compared to some other alternative flours, which is great for baking and desserts.

1. Combine the sugar, flour, salt, and baking powder in a bowl.
2. In a separate large bowl, whisk together the eggs and milk. Add the dry ingredients, in two additions, whisking to combine after each addition.
3. Transfer the mixture to a piping bag without a tip.
4. Heat a deep fryer to 375°F/190°C. Cut a small hole in the tip of the piping bag and pipe the batter directly into the frying oil to make layered circles (see photo for reference). Let fry, flipping as needed, until both sides are golden brown, about 3 minutes.
5. Use a spider or tongs to remove the funnel cakes from the oil, and transfer to a paper towel-lined sheet pan to drain.
6. Dust with confectioners' sugar while still hot and serve right away.

APPLE FRITTERS

Makes 1 dozen

There are apple orchards all over the Hudson Valley where I live, and so you can imagine that we love apple desserts. These fried fritters are a great addition to your apple repertoire, especially with the addition of spelt flour for some extra nutrients to help balance the deep-fried exterior.

3 medium-sized apples, any variety
.9oz/25 g eggs, room temperature
.9 oz/25 g egg yolks, room temperature
7.9 oz/225 g sour cream
1 oz/28 g milk, room temperature
.4 oz/12 g grapeseed oil
3/4 tsp/4 g kosher salt
2.6 oz/75 g sugar
7.9 oz/225 g spelt flour
1½ tsp/7 g baking powder
½ tsp/2 g ground all spice
1 tsp/5 g ground cinnamon

Vegetable oil, as needed for frying
Confectioners' sugar, as needed

1. Without peeling, grate each apple using the largest holes on a box grater or grating attachment. Over a bowl to catch the liquid, squeeze the apples in a clean towel to remove as much of the liquid as possible. Reserve any juice to drink, and set aside the shredded apples.
2. In a large bowl, mix the eggs, yolks, sour cream, milk, and oil. In another bowl, sift together the salt, sugar, flour, baking powder, allspice, and cinnamon.
3. Add the dry ingredients to the wet ingredients and mix just until homogenous. Add the reserved apples and fold in gently to distribute.
4. Transfer to an oiled bowl, cover, and rest for 20 minutes.
5. Heat a deep fryer or heavy-bottom pot filled halfway with oil to 365°F/185°C.
6. Use a 2 oz scoop (or ¼ cup measure) to deposit the batter into the hot oil. Fry, turning as needed, until golden brown all over, about 1 minute per side. Remove with a spider or heat-safe slotted spoon and transfer to a cooling rack to cool slightly.
7. Fill a shallow bowl with sugar to about ½-in deep. Toss the warm fritters in the sugar to coat.

BULGAR WHEAT PEANUT BUTTER TRUFFLES

Makes about 90 truffles

1 lb 5.2 oz/600 g water
5.2 oz/150 g bulgur
¼ tsp/2 g ground coriander
10.2 oz/290 g pitted dates
4.2 oz/118 g cocoa powder
.3 oz/8 g kosher salt
3.5 oz/100 g unsalted butter
14.5 oz/412 g peanut butter
Tempered dark (66%) chocolate or
   melted coating chocolate, as needed for
   coating

I use peanuts a lot. They are delicious, but they also use less water than any other nut to produce. Peanuts are also useful in farming as a rotation crop, to improve the soil where they are grown, and are usable from root to hull. I paired the peanuts, here in butter form, with bulgur wheat, a versatile ancient grain that itself lends a nutty, earthy flavor.

1. In a medium pot, bring the water and coriander to a boil. Add the bulgur and cook until the grains are tender, about 12 minutes. Drain and lay on a baking sheet to dry. Add the butter while still hot and mix to combine. Cool to room temperature.
2. Transfer the bulgur to a food processor and add the dates, cocoa powder, salt, butter, and peanut butter. Blend until mostly smooth.
3. Roll the mixture into ½ oz/15 g balls. You can also measure as a heaping teaspoon. Transfer to a silicone-lined baking sheet as done. Transfer to the refrigerator to chill for at least an hour and up to overnight.
4. Pour the tempered chocolate into a shallow dish and roll each truffle to lightly coat. Return to the baking sheet and let set before serving.

TEFF CRÊPES

Makes 10 servings

Teff flour is not a popular ingredient, but it happens to be an ancient grain that is naturally gluten-free, not to mention the health benefits that come with eating grains. It is a mild grain, with an earthy, sweet flavor. I like using brown teff for the color, but you can also use ivory teff.

3.7 oz/105 g brown teff flour
1.3 oz/37 g confectioners' sugar
1.8 oz/52 g eggs
1 oz/29 g egg yolks
10.1 oz/287 g milk

1. In a medium bowl, combine the flour and confectioners' sugar. In a separate bowl, blend the eggs, egg yolks, and milk.
2. Slowly add the egg mixture to the dry ingredients, whisking until there are no lumps. Cover and refrigerate overnight.
3. To prepare the crêpes, heat a small non-stick pan over medium heat. Add enough batter to just cover the bottom of the pan, tilting the pan as needed to spread to the edges.
4. Cook until the crêpe is lightly golden brown and releases from the pan, about 1 1/2 minutes. Carefully flip the crêpe and cook an additional minute, until the crêpe is set on both sides.
5. Transfer to a baking sheet to cool before serving.

TEFF CEREAL

Makes 8 servings

3.2 oz/90 g egg whites
2.9 oz/83 g teff
5.4 oz/152 g sugar
1 tsp/6 g kosher salt

Cereal has become dessert at my house, but it's so often less healthy than I would prefer. I wanted to do something about it, so I tried this version with brown teff flour. There is still some sugar, but now the cereal is more nutrient-dense and filling. Plus, you can make any shape you would like with cookie cutters. And don't throw away the scraps. I bake them and crumble them over ice cream or as a crunchy addition to anything sweet.

1. Preheat the oven to 400°F/200°C. Generously grease 2 baking sheets.
2. In a large bowl or stand mixer fitted with the paddle attachment, whip the egg whites to stiff peaks. Fold in the teff, sugar, and salt until just combined.
3. Spread the mixture on the prepared baking sheets. Bake until crispy, 8 to 12 minutes.
4. Remove from the oven and cut into your preferred shape. Set aside to cool.

ANCIENT GRAIN PRETZELS

Makes about 30 pretzels

It's no secret by now that I love grains, and this pretzel recipe is made with 100% ancient grains—which is rare. One concern with alternative flours is sometimes the finished texture, but these pretzels have a tender bread mouthfeel that you'll love.

1. In the bowl of a mixer fitted with the hook attachment, place the milk and eggs. Add the flours, yeast, salt, and sugar.

2. Mix on low speed for 3 minutes, then increase to medium speed for an additional 3 minutes. At this point, a small piece of the dough should stretch to form a thin "window" without breaking. If not, mix for an additional minute and test again.

3. Add the butter and continue to mix until a stiff dough has formed, about 2 minutes. Transfer to an oiled bowl and set aside for 40 minutes to ferment.

4. Divide the dough into 1.8 oz/50 g pieces and pre-shape into logs. Rest for 10 minutes.

5. Roll the logs into 10-inch lengths and shape into a pretzel.

6. Preheat the oven to 425°F/218°C.

7. Dip each pretzel in a lye solution, and sprinkle with coarse salt. Transfer to a parchment paper-lined baking sheet.

8. Bake, with steam if possible, until the pretzels are golden brown all over and fully baked, about 20 minutes.

1 lb /454 gmilk
3 large eggs
1 lb 2 oz/510 g emmer flour
1 lb 2 oz/510 g durum flour
2 ¾ tsp/8 g instant dry yeast
.5 oz/16 g kosher salt
2 oz/58 g sugar
4 oz/113 g unsalted butter, soft

To prepare a lye solution, boil 1½ quarts of water and add 2 oz of food-grade lye. Add ½ quart of cold water to cool it down before using.

Always use gloves and protective eyewear when using lye solutions.

If you would prefer to use a baking soda solution, mix about ¼ cup baking soda to every 4 cups of water. Pretzels using baking soda will not be as brown or glossy as those using lye.

KOGINUT SQUASH GOURDS

Makes about 4 dozen rolls

11.5 oz/325 g Koginut squash, seeded
   and roughly chopped
2 tbsp/30 mL olive oil
Kosher salt, as needed

1 lb 7.7 oz/672 g milk
7 oz/200 g eggs
½ oz/16 g sorghum syrup
3 lb 6.7 oz/1.55 kg durum flour
12.5 oz/354 g spelt flour
.78 oz/22 g dry yeast
1.2 oz/34 g kosher salt
4.8 oz/136 g sugar
5.6 oz/160 g unsalted butter, softened

Egg Wash (page 196), as needed

The combination of durum and spelt is my favorite when substituting for traditional wheat flour. Durum has higher protein than traditional wheat flour, but can also last for up to 2 years, where conventional wheat flour has a short shelf life of 8 months. I add squash here for a beautiful color, but also an added boost of nutrients and sweetness.

1. Preheat the oven to 400°F/205°C. Toss the squash with olive oil, season with salt, and spread on a baking sheet. Roast until the squash is golden brown and tender.
2. Transfer to a blender or food processor and process until smooth, adding a splash of water or broth as needed to facilitate blending. Cool before using.
3. In the bowl of a stand-mixer fitted with the dough hook, add the squash, milk, eggs, and sorghum. Add the flours, yeast, salt, and sugar, and mix on low speed for about three minutes. Increase the speed to medium and mix for an additional three minutes.
4. Remove a small piece of dough from the mixer and gently stretch it to form a thin "window" of dough. If the dough breaks or does not hold a window easily, mix for an additional 2 minutes or so until the dough is developed enough to stretch without breaking.
5. Add the butter and continue to mix on medium speed for 2 minutes.
6. Transfer the dough to an oiled bowl and set aside to ferment for 40 minutes.
7. Divide the dough into 50 g pieces and shape into loose rounds. Set aside to rest for 10 minutes.
8. Shape the rolls again into tighter rounds.
9. On a work surface, lay four pieces of 5-in/13-cm twine so that they cross over each other in the center. Place a piece of dough where the twine intersects and brush the top of the dough with egg wash. Bring the twine up around the dough and tie loosely.
10. Transfer to a parchment paper-lined baking sheet and set aside in a warm place to proof, about 1 hour.
11. Preheat an oven to 425°F/218°C. Bake, with steam if possible, until the pretzels are golden brown and fully baked, about 20 minutes. Transfer to racks to cool, and remove the twine before serving.

SPELT FOCACCIA

Makes two 12-in by 6-in loaves

I like to make some brands by hand, and this focaccia is one of them. The dough is very forgiving and loves the gentle hand-mix. Because our hands are not as powerful as an electric mixer, it may take a little longer, but it's worth the wait. I've used spelt flour here for a boost of nutrition and a really lovely flavor.

1. Prepare the Biga 18 hours before mixing the final dough. In a covered container, combine the flour, water, and yeast, and mix until well-combined. Set aside to ferment overnight.
2. For the dough, transfer the biga to a large mixing bowl and add water, olive oil, and sorghum syrup. Mix by hand until the biga is broken down and the ingredients are mostly combined, about 5 minutes.
3. Add the flour, yeast, and salt, and continue to work the dough until a dough begins to form. It will be sticky and slightly wet.
4. Cover the bowl and set aside to ferment for 30 minutes. Fold the dough over on itself, then rest for another 30 minutes. Fold once more, and set aside for 10 minutes.
5. Cover the bottom of a small baking sheet with semolina. Divide the dough in two halves. Lightly shape into rounds, dip the bottom in the semolina dough, and transfer to a parchment paper-lined baking sheet. Brush with olive oil, and set aside for 10 minutes.
6. Transfer the dough to 6 – by 12-inch baking pans. Coat your hands in olive oil and stretch each round to the edges of the pan. Set aside in a humid area (or bread proofer) for 30 minutes.
7. Preheat the oven to 480°F/250°C.
8. Drizzle the dough with olive oil, and use your fingers to stipple the dough all over. If you would like to add toppings, add them at this stage.
9. Bake, with steam if possible, until the bread is golden brown all over, about 18 minutes.
10. Remove from the oven and brush with olive oil. Sprinkle with finishing salt and other toppings, as desired. Cool fully before serving.

BIGA PRE-FERMENT

5 oz/141 g spelt flour
2.9 oz/82 g water, room temperature
pinch/.1 g instant dry yeast

DOUGH

13.4 oz/380 g water
1.3 oz/38 g olive oil
.2 oz/5 g sorghum syrup
15.8 oz/448 g spelt flour
¾ tsp/2 g instant dry yeast
.5 oz/13 g kosher salt

Semolina, as needed
Olive oil, as needed
Coarse Maldon sea salt, as needed

SPELT AND SORGHUM PIZZA DOUGH

Makes 1 lb/454 g

4 oz/113 g spelt flour
½ tsp/.6 g instant yeast
½ tsp/2 g kosher salt
½ tsp/2 g sugar
1 tsp/6 g olive oil
¼ tsp/1.5 g sorghum syrup
2.4 oz/67 g water

Adding ancient grains to your dough is an instant Pizza Night upgrade. Not only are ancient grains good for our bodies, but spelt—one of the most ancient of the ancient grains—creates a nice and tender dough that makes for a crisp, chewy pizza crust.

1. In the bowl of a stand mixer, combine the flour, yeast, salt, sugar, olive oil, syrup, and water. Mix on low speed until a dough forms, about 4 minutes. Increase to medium-low speed and mix until the gluten has developed, but the dough is still slightly sticky, an additional 3 minutes.
2. Cover and set aside to ferment at room temperature for 30 minutes.
3. Remove from the bowl and shape into a round on a floured surface. Oil the round and place on a baking sheet. Cover and rest in the refrigerator overnight.
4. To use, remove from the refrigerator one hour before shaping. Roll out and top as desired. Bake in a 470°F oven until the edges are golden brown, 10 to 12 minutes.

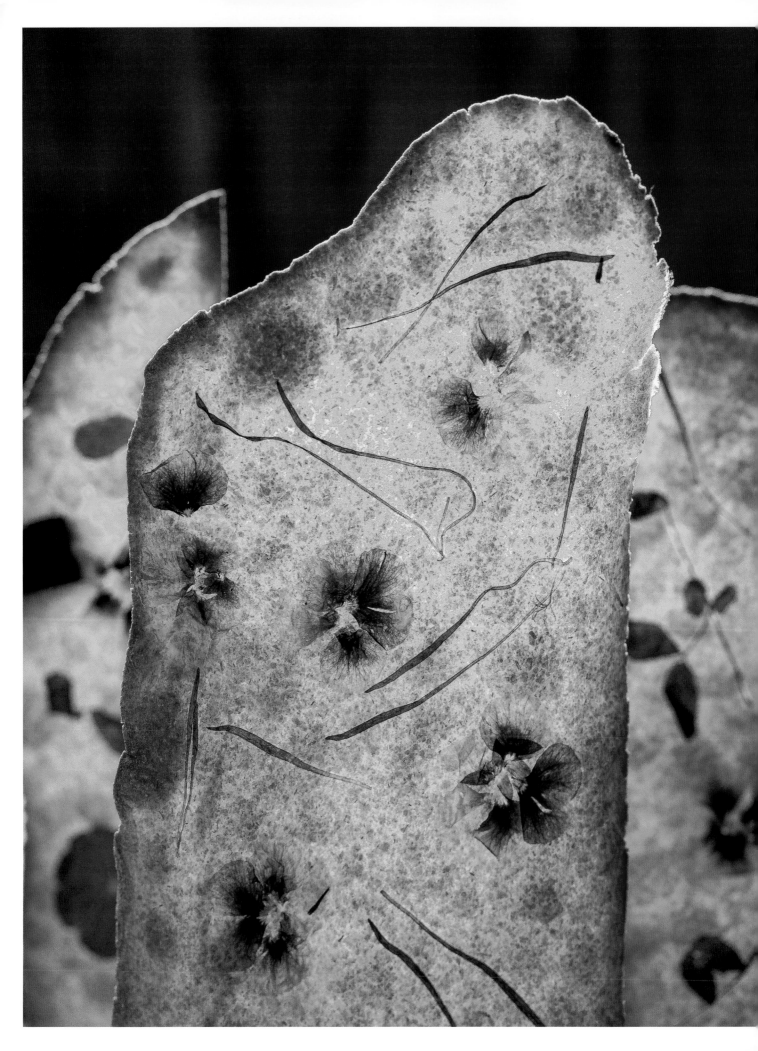

EINKORN LAVASH

Makes 5 pieces

Einkorn is an ancient grain—in fact, the most ancient grain we know of. I like it for a flat bread because it's mild and well-paired with an array of condiments, dips, and dishes. The boiled-potato water not only gives this vital resource a second life, but also adds a subtle flavor. Sorghum is used here where we might usually use molasses or maybe honey, to keep with the ancient grain vibe (it also enhances the flavor of the einkorn).

9 oz/255 g potato water (leftover from boiled potatoes)
oz/241 g milk
1 oz/28 g molasses
1 oz/28 g honey
.5 oz/15 g fresh yeast
1 lb 14 oz/850 g einkorn flour
.8 oz/24 g kosher salt
Edible flowers, as needed
Olive oil, as needed for finishing

1. In the bowl of a stand mixer fitted with the dough hook, combine the potato water, milk, molasses, honey, and yeast. Add the flour and salt. Mix on low speed for 10 minutes.
2. Divide the dough into 5 pieces. Transfer to a parchment paper-lined sheet pan, and transfer to a refrigerator to retard overnight.
3. Roll the dough very thin. Brush the dough with water and press the flowers onto the dough. Use a rolling pin to adhere the flowers to the dough.
4. Transfer to olive oiled sheet pans. Brush the tops of the lavash with oil and set aside to rest for 15 minutes.
5. Preheat the oven to 450°F/232°C. Bake until golden brown around the edges, about 7 minutes.

PUFFED QUINOA CHOCOLATE SHARDS

Makes 1 quart

7.3 oz/206 g 66% chocolate, melted
4.6 oz/130 g hazelnut paste
8.1 oz/230 g puffed quinoa
2 sheets rice paper
.4 oz/10 g Maldon sea salt

Quinoa is a seed, not a grain, but it is still categorized as an ancient grain thanks to its long cultivation history. While I love it for its nutrients, texture, and flavor, quinoa also happens to be a low-water crop that thrives in poor soil conditions. They flourish without any pesticides and help with soil erosion. What can't quinoa do? Well, it can pair with chocolate, and quinoa chocolate bars are my go-to. It is a crisp and crunchy bar that happens to be made with a superfood.

1. In a bowl, combine the chocolate, hazelnut paste, and quinoa.
2. On a silicone-lined baking sheet, place two sheets of rice paper, shiny side up.
3. Divide the chocolate mixture over both sheets of rice paper and sprinkle with salt. Let set until firm before breaking apart into shards.

SORGHUM SODA FLOAT WITH HONEY MALT ICE CREAM

Makes 6 to 8 servings

Sorghum is a grain that has a lot of great uses. I like to use the syrup form over corn syrup or molasses because it is a more environmentally-friendly cereal grain crop. It can adapt to heat or cold and protects our natural resources. Malt is also made from cereal grains. Barley is the most commonly used, but you can find malts made from wheat, rye, or oats.

1. In a saucepan, heat the milk and honey to a strong simmer.
2. In a medium heat-proof bowl, combine the yolks, malt powder, milk powder, and salt. While whisking the egg mixture, pour about ¼ of the milk mixture into the bowl and whisk well until combined. Stream the contents of the bowl back into the pot, whisking constantly, until combined.
3. Switch to a spoon and cook over low-medium heat until the ice cream base coats the back of a spoon. Remove from the heat and strain into a clean bowl. Set aside, stirring occasionally, until the mixture cools to room temperature.
4. Add the butter to the warm ice cream base and blend with an immersion blender until smooth. Cover and refrigerate overnight.
5. Process the ice cream according to the directions for your machine.
6. Meanwhile, prepare the soda base. Bring the water to a boil in a small saucepan. Remove from the heat and add the sorghum syrup. Set aside to cool.
7. To assemble the floats, place 3 scoops of ice cream in a large, chilled glass. Add about ¼ cup of the sorghum soda base and top with club soda. Adjust with more of the soda, as needed. Serve right away.

HONEY MALT ICE CREAM
2 lb/1000 g milk
1 lb 1.6 oz/500 g honey
4.2 oz/120 g malt powder
1.8 oz/50 g milk powder
½ tsp/2.5 g kosher salt

7 oz/200 g egg yolks
4.4 oz/125 g softened butter

Sorghum Soda Base
3.5 oz/100 g water
10.6 oz/300 g sorghum syrup

Club soda, as needed for serving

BARLEY PUDDING WITH RHUBARB COMPOTE

Makes 6 to 8 servings

PUDDING

15.2 oz/431 g milk
4 oz hulled barley
1.3 oz/38 g brown sugar
¾ tsp/4 g kosher salt
2.1 oz/60 g crème fraiche
4½ oz heavy cream, whipped to soft
  peaks

RHUBARB COMPOTE

10.6 oz/300 g roughly chopped rhubarb
2.8 oz/80 g sugar
.4 oz/10 g lemon juice

Balsamic Del Cristo Traditional, or
  other high-quality balsamic vinegar
Gaillardia (Blanket Flowers), as needed
  for garnish

I love rice pudding, but rice is not the only grain worthy of the pudding treatment. I love barley in this pudding because it has a chewy texture, versus the softer rice in traditional rice pudding. Adding crème fraiche cuts the sweetness with a little tang, and then the rhubarb compote finishes the job with a great sour acidity. The drizzle of sweet and acidic balsamic vinegar is optional, but I never leave it off.

1. In a heavy-bottom saucepot, bring the milk, barley, brown sugar, and salt to a boil. Reduce to a simmer and cook, stirring occasionally, until the barley is tender but still chewy, about 1 hour.
2. Remove from the heat and pour the pudding on a baking sheet. Set aside, stirring occasionally, until cooled.
3. Meanwhile, make the rhubarb compote. Combine the rhubarb and sugar in a saucepot until the rhubarb is tender, about 10 minutes. Remove from the heat, add lemon juice, and cool.
4. Transfer the pudding to a large bowl, and fold in the crème fraiche and whipped cream.
5. Fill serving glasses about 2/3 full of pudding. Top with rhubarb compote and a drizzle of Balsamic Del Cristo Traditional, and top with a gaillardia.

Chapter 5: Pantry

THIS CHAPTER IS FULL OF SOME OF my most frequently used recipes, like my go-to Apple Cider Vinegar (page 192) and savory Tallow Puff Pastry (page 199). Using food waste to create something you might otherwise buy at a grocery store is a small change that can make a big impact. You'll see these recipes used in other desserts throughout this book, but they have applications in your every day cooking and baking.

APPLE CIDER VINEGAR

Makes 1 pint

2.8 oz/80 g apple peels, any variety
.6 oz/18 g sugar
11.2 oz/317 g water

Apples are a New York-grown staple, used in desserts, savory dishes, and of course, eaten out of hand. The peels are often discarded, which is a tragedy considering you can use them to make fresh apple cider vinegar. You'll find this vinegar in many recipes in this book, but it also has countless other uses.

1. In a large jar, combine the apple peels, sugar, and water. Cover with a tight-fitting lid and shake until the sugar is distributed and begins to dissolve.
2. Remove the lid and recover the jar with a swatch of clean cloth or double-layered cheesecloth, and secure in place with a rubber band or tightly-tied kitchen twine.
3. Place the jar in a dark spot, like a kitchen cabinet or pantry, for 3 to 4 weeks. It should be slightly bubbly. Shake or stir the contents of the jar every few days, making sure the apples are fully submerged.
4. After the initial 3 to 4 weeks, strain the mixture. Compost the apple pieces and return the liquid to the jar. Return the cloth cover and place in a dark place for another 3 to 4 weeks until it smells pungent, like vinegar.
5. The vinegar is now ready to use or store.

CHIFFON FLOUR

Makes about 1 lb/454 g

1 lb/454 g scraps from baked cakes

Cake scraps are just a reality in bakeshops. We already have some great uses for these pieces—cake pops, rum balls, or sometimes in a Danish filling—but I wondered if you could reuse cake to make more cake. The answer is yes, and you'll find this flour in some of the recipes earlier in this book where it adds the structure of all-purpose flour with a little extra flavor (and less waste!).

1. Preheat the oven to 300°F/150°C.
2. Spread the cake scraps on a baking sheet and bake in the oven until dry, about 30 minutes. Let cool.
3. Transfer the cooled scraps to a blender or food processor, and blend until the cake forms a fine powder. Sift and re-blend any larger pieces until they are fine. Store in a tightly-covered container until needed.

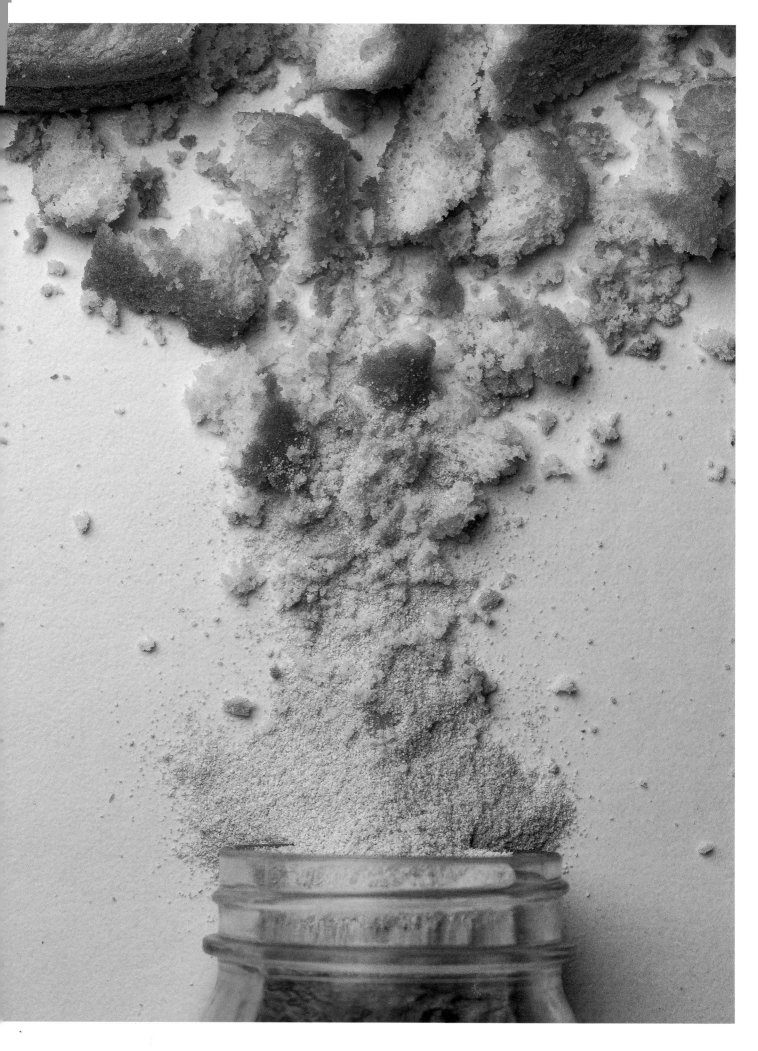

FLAX SEED PASTE

Makes enough to replace 1 whole egg

This mixture is a 1:3 ratio of flax to water, and can be increased as needed.

1.2 oz/33 g flax seed
3.5 oz/100 g water

1. Combine the flax and water in a blender and blend until smooth.

CURED EGG YOLKS

Makes 6 yolks

Cured egg yolks are one of my favorite things to do with yolks. Once cured, they become firm, so you can shave or grate the yolk on a brownie or even use it as an inclusion in a cookie. It adds richness and a little saltiness to any dish.

10.6 oz/300 g sugar
10.6 oz/300 g kosher salt
6 egg yolks

1. In a shallow vessel, combine half the sugar and half the salt. Spread to cover the bottom of the dish, and make six shallow depressions in the mixture.
2. Carefully transfer the egg yolks to the vessel, settling each into one of the depressions.
3. In a small bowl, combine the remaining sugar and salt. Sprinkle this mixture over the egg yolks to coat evenly.
4. Wrap the dish tightly and transfer to the refrigerator.
5. Cure the yolks for 6 days. When ready, remove the yolks from the sugar and salt mixture, and gently wipe any remaining salt from the yolks with a damp towel.
6. Store the yolks in an air-tight container for up to a month.

EGG WASH

Makes 1 cup/237 mL

This is a basic egg wash recipe for finishing pastries and other baked goods, responsible for the golden brown glossy sheen that makes some foods so appealing. If you don't use the whole batch, you can freeze it in between projects.

4 whole eggs
3 egg yolks
1/2 oz/10 g milk
¼ tsp/2 g kosher salt

1. In a bowl or container, combine the eggs, yolks, milk, and salt. Use an immersion blender to blend to a smooth liquid. The egg wash can also be made in a tabletop blender. Refrigerate in a covered container until needed.

WILDFLOWER SIMPLE SYRUP

Makes 1 lb 3 oz/550 g

For ages, flowers have played some part in the human diet, but over the years, they've become almost exclusively decorative. To me, flowers are beautiful and bountiful, with great flavor and vitamins and nutrients. Here, they are steeped in syrup to use for cakes and other desserts, but also lemonade, tea, and cocktails.

7.1 oz/200 g water
5.3 oz/150 g wildflowers (read more about edible flowers on page 112)
7.1 oz/200 g sugar

1. In a saucepot, bring the water to a light simmer. Remove from the heat, add the flowers, and set aside to steep, about 8 minutes.
2. Strain the flowers and return the water to the pot. Add the sugar and bring to a boil, stirring until the sugar dissolves.
3. Remove from the heat and cool fully. Refrigerate in a tightly sealed container until needed.

TALLOW PUFF PASTRY

Makes 2 lb/907 g

Tallow is the fat from rendered beef or mutton. In restaurants, tallow most often comes from beef, and it is frequently discarded simply because there is such an overabundance of it. Rather than waste what is a flavorful and inexpensive ingredient, I've used it in place of high-price butter to roll into puff pastry dough. When baked, it has the familiar texture and appearance, with a rich, more savory flavor that I love for pot pies or savory pastries.

DOUGH
10 oz/283 g ice cold water
1 lb/454 g bread flour
4 oz /113 gpastry flour
½ oz/14 g kosher salt
4 oz/113 g beef tallow, room temperature (should be soft)

ROLL-IN BUTTER BLOCK
Bread flour, as needed
1 lb 2 oz/510 g beef tallow, cold

1. For the dough, place the water in the bowl of a stand mixer fitted with the dough hook. Add the flours and salt, then the tallow.
2. Mix on low speed until a dough begins to form. Stop the mixer and turn the dough over in the bowl, and then continue mixing until the dough is just homogenous.
3. Transfer the dough to a silicone-lined baking sheet and press into a 12-in by 8-in rectangle. Refrigerate for 20 minutes.
4. Meanwhile, prepare the roll-in tallow block. Dust your work surface with flour. Place the tallow on the surface and dust with flour. Pound the tallow with a rolling pin until pliable. Shape to a rectangle that is about half the size of the dough. It will be about ½-in thick.
5. Remove the dough from the refrigerator and place on the work surface. Brush any flour from the top of the dough.
6. Using a dowl rod or other tool, mark a line down the center of the dough.
7. Place the prepared tallow roll-in block on one half of the dough, to the left of the line. Fold the other side of the dough over the tallow to cover, and carefully pinch the overlapping dough to form a seal.
8. Preform a 4-fold on the dough: roll the dough to 9-in by 20-inches. It should be no less than ½-inch thick. Transfer to a sheet pan and refrigerate for 20 to 25 minutes.
9. Perform a 3-fold: roll the dough to 12 – by 18-inches, and no less than ½-inch thick. Fold the right side of the dough to just past center, and then fold the left side to cover and meet the other end, like folding a letter. Transfer to a sheet pan and refrigerate for 20 to 25 minutes.
10. Perform one additional 4-fold and one additional 3-fold, chilling for 20 to 25 minutes in between. Wrap and refrigerate overnight, or until needed.

DATE PIT "COFFEE"

Makes 4 servings

Pitting dates is a labor of love, and there is no sense in wasting any of that effort. I love the almost chocolate coffee flavor that comes through when the date pits are roasted and ground, used to create a coffee-like beverage that is really satisfying (with no caffeine, too). You can save date pits in the freezer until you have enough to use.

3.5 oz/100 g date pits
1 lb 13 oz/826 g water

1. Preheat an oven to 325° F. Spread the pits on a baking sheet and roast until slightly browned and dry, about 10 minutes. Remove from the oven and set aside to cool.
2. Transfer the pits to a food processor or spice grinder, and process to a fine powder. This can be done in one batch or for individual servings.
3. To brew, bring the water to a simmer and add powder. Remove from the heat and steep for 5 minutes. Strain through a reusable coffee filter, if available, or a sieve double-lined with paper filters.

SOUR MILK CHEESE

Makes 4 lb 6 oz/2 kg

It's a common problem: the milk container is just too big for our needs, and the milk goes sour. Different from spoiled milk (which you will know if you taste it), soured milk is still safe to drink and can be used just like milk for an extra tang.

4 lb 2.7 oz/1.89 kg milk
2.4 oz/68 g Apple Cider Vinegar (page 192)

1. Bring the milk to a boil in a heavy-bottomed saucepot. Reduce the heat to low and stir in the vinegar. Remove from the heat. The mixture will begin to separate into solids and liquid.
2. Line a large fine-mesh sieve with cheesecloth. Strain the milk mixture. The finished cheese will be a little bit firmer than a typical ricotta, but still soft.
3. Transfer to a covered container and refrigerate until ready to use.

BOURBON WHISKEY CARAMEL

Makes 11 oz/331 g

This sauce is used in the Chestnut Tart with Turban Squash Diplomat Cream (page 112) recipe, but you'll find yourself using it over and over. Spoon it over ice cream, drizzle on other cakes, or dip apple segments for a little sweet treat.

5.3 oz/150 g sugar
5.3 oz/150 g heavy cream, room temperature
.4 oz/11 g whiskey
½ tsp/3 g fleur de sel

1. Heat the sugar in a medium saucepan over medium heat. Cook, swirling the pan occasionally, until the sugar has melted and turned a deep amber color, about 5 minutes.
2. Add the cream, stirring to combine. The cream will bubble up in the pan, so add in a few additions, if needed. Remove from the heat and add the whiskey and salt.
3. Cool before refrigerating until needed.

ONION POWDER

Makes about ¼ cup

Professional kitchens use tons of onions, and the skin is nearly always discarded as unusable trim. While this onion peel powder may seem like a big effort for a small outcome, every little bit counts toward a better planet. Plus, onion peels hold lots of antioxidants, making this a total no-brainer.

5 cups/1.2 mL dry onion skins

1. Separate the layers, discarding any damaged peels. Plunge the skins in cold water, removing any dirt and debris. Repeat at least one more time, or until the skins are very clean. Pat dry with a clean towel.
2. Transfer to baking sheets in even layers. Set the oven to 150º F (or as low as possible) and dry the skins until they are very dry and brittle, about 3 hours. You can also use a dehydrator.
3. Blend in a small spice grinder, working in batche as needed, or in a large high-powered blender for best results.